UNCOVERING

1 CORINTHIANS 11

Does It Apply Today?

Jeremy Howard

TABLE OF CONTENTS

Introduction

What would you think if you were told that there was a portion of the Bible that, although it was never lost, was ignored for decades? If you are a strong, Bible-believing Christian, I suppose you would get defensive at first (I'm sure I would, too), but eventually you may want to know more about this text.

Something like this happened in Josiah's day as described in 2 Kings 22. Josiah was a king who cared about the things of the Lord and wanted to serve Him well. One day, Hilkiah, the high priest, discovered a text that had been in the temple for a long time, but it had been set aside and forgotten. The text was the Torah—Genesis through Deuteronomy—containing inspired revelation. It was the Law that Israel was to observe. Judah was in such bad condition that they were living without their foundational, inspired document.

Shaphan, a scribe, took hold of this vital text and brought it to King Josiah, saying, "Hilkiah the priest has given me a book," (v. 10). *A book*? What irony. This Jewish scribe did not realize that the most important document he could ever study or copy down was right there in his hand. Shaphan proceeded to read the book for Josiah.

Upon hearing the Law, the king tore his clothes and lamented. He exclaimed, "Great is the wrath of the Lord that burns against us, because our fathers have not listened to the words of this book, to do according to all that is written concerning us," (v. 13). The Lord heard Josiah's cry and enabled him to enact a variety of reforms in Judah, promoting lawful living among the people.

Josiah's response to recovering God's ignored revelation is exemplary. All of God's people should deeply desire to embrace every word from God; our desire should be to feast on every word that comes from His mouth.

In many ways, 1 Corinthians 11:2–16 has been a "lost book" for the church in recent generations. Even though this passage is not as foundational to biblical theology as the Torah, and even though it has not been as abandoned as the Torah was in Josiah's day, the fact remains that it is often ignored, sometimes suppressed, and rarely embraced. It has been dismissed as too difficult, too culturally conditioned, and too unique. It has led many to wonder, "Is it possible for Christians to actually understand this passage and make application today?" The answer is Yes!

In August 2021, I had to reckon with this passage. For the 15 years of my Christian life that had preceded that time, I did my best to sidestep the topic of head coverings and hair lengths any time it would come up. "There's only one passage about it," I'd say; or, "We don't fully understand all of the cultural principles at play." But these common retorts will not do when one is charged with faithfully preaching through Scripture, verse-by-verse and chapter-by-chapter.

I was a year into preaching through 1 Corinthians and this passage was up next. What would I say? All I could do was exegete the text—and honest exegesis has a way of tearing down man's attempts to avoid what God has said. This short book is the fruit of that effort.

There is a great deal at stake in this endeavor. This passage is critical to arriving at a sound theology of gender roles in the church and of headship and authority. (There is a reason why Joyce Meyer never preaches this passage!) Further, this passage is a great test of our commitment to consistent hermeneutics. Quite often, otherwise-sound Bible teachers change their interpretive grid when dealing with this passage. We must consider why this is and seek to be consistent with our own interpretive methods.

I have written this to call you to heed the word of God, even though it may seem foreign or strange. First, I will start by examining the text, offering conclusive observations with notes to back up my claims. I am not presenting this material in verse-by-verse exposition like a commentary—there are plenty of those already! Rather, I am presenting this material in more of a debate format. This is not because I want to be divisive about this issue; rather, my goal is to persuade you of the continuing significance of Paul's inspired instruction to the church. I hope that this format is more efficient at addressing the key points.

Next, I will answer common objections and seek to make application to today. I have also included two appendices that I hope are particularly helpful for church leaders as they wrestle with this passage. This is a difficult text to discuss in the modern age, but Bible teachers must do it—and it does not have to divide a church.

I find it fascinating that most sound Bible readers, commentators, and preachers understand the majority of the apostle's instructions in this passage. It was written plainly enough. However, when considering modern-day application and significance, there are endless paths people have taken to avoid modern-day significance. Some will disagree with my conclusions on the basis of their own exegetical work. If a person has wrestled with the text and he or she has a clear conscience before God, it is not my job to judge; nevertheless, each one must deal with the text. I desire each one of us to embrace the spirit of Josiah in desiring to listen to the word of God. We must all seek to choose fear of God over fear of man and submissively hear the Lord's instruction.

Before we read the text and begin to examine it together, I want to share with you seven basic beliefs about the Bible and our hearts toward it. This is the same list I shared with our congregation before I preached through the passage in 2021, and it is vital for us to keep this in mind as we work through the text.

Jeremy Howard

October 2022

1. **The Bible is the word of God.** God has spoken and He has preserved His message. The Bible is not just any other book.

2. **The Bible has full authority over me.** All of our thinking and living must be directed by the sufficient word of God.

3. **The Bible is understandable.** There are varying degrees of difficulty in interpreting passages, but God has spoken in such a way that we can understand and obey.

4. **The Bible should not be apologized for.** No Christian should be embarrassed by what God has said or seek to placate contemporary culture in lieu of obeying God.

5. **Honesty with the text must be the goal.** False witness is an abomination; therefore, hearing and adhering to the word of God is the only acceptable aim.

6. **Feelings never justify the rejection of a text.** We must fear God above all other fears. If the clear meaning of a text seems "weird" to us, there is certainly a problem with us, not Scripture.

7. **Willingness to obey precedes interpretation.** We must be willing to follow God even when we are unsure where He is taking us.

1 Corinthians 11

²Now I praise you because you remember me in everything and hold firmly to the traditions, just as I delivered them to you. ³But I want you to understand that Christ is the head of every man, and the man is the head of a woman, and God is the head of Christ. ⁴Every man who has *something* on his head while praying or prophesying disgraces his head. ⁵But every woman who has her head uncovered while praying or prophesying disgraces her head, for she is one and the same as the woman whose head is shaved. ⁶For if a woman does not cover her head, let her also have her hair cut off; but if it is disgraceful for a woman to have her hair cut off or her head shaved, let her cover her head. ⁷For a man ought not to have his head covered, since he is the image and glory of God; but the woman is the glory of man. ⁸For man does not originate from woman, but woman from man; ⁹for indeed man was not created for the woman's sake, but woman for the man's sake. ¹⁰Therefore the woman ought to have *a symbol of* authority on her head, because of the angels. ¹¹However, in the Lord, neither is woman independent of man, nor is man independent of woman. ¹²For as the woman originates from the man, so also

the man *has his birth* through the woman; and all things originate from God. [13] Judge for yourselves: is it proper for a woman to pray to God *with her head* uncovered? [14] Does not even nature itself teach you that if a man has long hair, it is a dishonor to him, [15] but if a woman has long hair, it is a glory to her? For her hair is given to her for a covering. [16] But if one is inclined to be contentious, we have no other practice, nor have the churches of God.

(NASB 1995)

Notes and Conclusions about the Text

In this section, certain observations about the text will be made that limit the scope of possible interpretations and applications. The goal is to apply sound principles of exegesis so that the original intended meaning of the author comes forth and is recognized.

1. **Paul's threefold use of "head" in v. 3 refers to authority, not "origin" or "source," as some have argued.**

   ◆ "Origin" and "source" need not be completely separated from "authority," as one's relationship to authority is tied to one's origin in one way or another. However, Paul's point in this chapter was to recognize and illustrate authority and order in God's church.

   ◆ Wayne Grudem does a thorough job defending the view that Paul had authority in view.[1] The popular Greek

---

[1] Wayne Grudem, "Does Κεφαλή ('Head') Mean 'Source' Or 'Authority Over' in Greek Literature? A Survey of 2,336 Examples," *Trinity Journal* ns 6.1 (Spring 1985), 38–59. Against strong evidence detailed in the vast majority of Greek lexicons, Gordon Fee counters Grudem's argument in his

lexicon BDAG states that the Greek word for "head," κεφαλή (*kephalē*), is used "to denote superior rank" among living beings, citing 1 Corinthians 11:3 in its definition.[2] Mike Winger has laid out a thorough and popular-level defense of *kephalē* as authority based on a variety of Greek lexicons on his YouTube channel.[3]

◆ Paul's use of *kephalē* in reference to authority (especially the authority of Christ) is consistent in the New Testament. Ephesians 1:22, 4:15, and Colossians 2:10 are examples of this use.

◆ Later in the letter, the apostle highlighted the authority of Christ over all things, along with His submission to the Father (15:22–27). Interpreting *kephalē* as "authority" here in chapter 11 helps the reader recognize one of the over-arching themes of the letter: authority and order within God's design (5:1–5, 6:3–4, 14:33, 40, 15:23).

2. "Christ" in v. 3 refers to the incarnate Son of God.

◆ The Son of God made flesh is the head of every man. Following His earthly life and death, Jesus Christ "was declared the Son of God with power by the resurrection

---

popular commentary. See Gordon D. Fee, *The First Epistle to the Corinthians*, Revised Edition (Grand Rapids: Eerdmans, 2014), 552–557.

[2] BDAG: William Danker and Walter Bauer, "κεφαλή," *A Greek-English Lexicon of the New Testament and Other Early Christian Literature*, 3rd Edition (Chicago: University of Chicago Press, 2000), 542.

[3] Mike Winger, "Male Headship: Is it REALLY Biblical? Women in Ministry part 8," YouTube: https://youtu.be/pHxJblq_Fdc, Accessed August 2022.

from the dead," (Romans 1:4) and is the Man through whom the world will be judged, His appointment being proven through the resurrection (Acts 17:31). Without a doubt, Jesus Christ incarnate is the Lord (or, "head") of every man.

- In a special sense, Christ rules over all people in His Church. He currently rules as King of His church (Colossians 1:13, 18, Revelation 1:6), and the Christian confession is that Jesus Christ is the Apostle and High Priest of salvation (Hebrews 3:1), as well as the Chief Shepherd (1 Peter 5:4).

- Jesus Christ, in His perpetual humanity, has the Father as His *kephalē*—His authoritative head. It was in the incarnation that God the Son first submitted to God the Father, as Jesus made it clear that He came to do the Father's will (John 4:34, 6:38, 15:10b). In this sense, God (the Father) is the "head" of Christ (the Son). This authority-submission relationship in no way causes the Son to be inferior to the Father in nature; They share in the same divine substance and are equally the one, true God. The Son freely came (Philippians 2:5–8) and He freely submits to the Father (John 5:30).

3. Man's headship over woman at least refers to marriage.

- In v. 3, the apostle wrote, "the man is the head of a woman." It cannot be known for certain if Paul had all men and women in view or husbands and wives only. In the New Testament, the same Greek word is used to refer to men and husbands, and the same Greek word is used to refer to women and wives. The context of each word's usage determines the translation. Translators of the *English Standard Version* believe husbands and wives are in view as that translation renders v. 3, "the head of a wife is her husband."[4]

+ There are a variety of reasons to believe that Paul had the husband-wife relationship in view, as opposed to all men and women generally. Below are some reasons why a person may interpret the text that way.

  ▷ The Greek ἀνήρ (*anēr*) means "man" or "husband," and γυνή (*gunē*) means "woman" or "wife." These are the words used in v. 3 when Paul said, "the man is the head of a woman." He spoke of "man" and "woman" in the singular, potentially teaching that just one man is the head over just one woman. Elsewhere, Paul spoke of men and women in the assembly generally using plural forms (1 Timothy 2:8–10); that is not the case here, which may indicate that the marital relationship is in view. Furthermore, dozens of times in the New Testament the singular *anēr* is used with the definite article, as here in v. 3, and in each instance,

---

[4] It is possible that this translation decision was driven by a view of the covering as a cultural symbol of being engaged or married. Regardless, the ESV and the NRSV are the only two major English translations that use the terms "husband" and "wife" in v. 3.

the author is speaking of one individual man or husband. First Corinthians 11 would have to be the exceptional case. Though interesting, the significance of this is debatable.

▷ If Paul sought to indicate all males and all females, it is conceivable that he would have used alternative Greek words for those designations, like the adjectival *arrén* and *thélus*, respectively. Paul used these words in Romans 1:26–27 and Galatians 3:28. Once again, this is an interesting observation with debatable significance.

▷ Further on in the passage (vv. 7–10), the Genesis narrative is drawn upon, which is not only the revelation of humanity's beginning, but the foundation for understanding the marital relationship. Eve was not created to be the helper of all men, but she was created to be her husband's helper in particular, one of the major contributions being child-bearing in the marital context. With this in view, some commentators even state that a woman *becomes* "the glory of man" (v. 7) only when she is joined to a husband.[5]

---

[5] For instance, David Lowery states, "A woman's (a wife's) glory and image was derived from and complementary to that of the man (her husband). Man, then, was God's authoritative representative who found in woman a divinely-made ally in fulfilling this role. In this sense she as a wife is the glory of man, her husband," in "1 Corinthians," *The Bible Knowledge*

14

> ▷ Aside from the possibility here in this passage, the New Testament never teaches that men are the authoritative head of women generally; however, it is explicitly taught that husbands are the heads of their wives (Ephesians 5:22–25). This fact has presumably driven many commentators to interpret Paul as referencing husbands and wives in vv. 3, 5, and 7–9.[6]

> ▷ Later on in the letter, when addressing the proper behavior of women in corporate worship, Paul spoke specifically to wives, as the following verse indicates when he instructed them to consult with "their own husbands at home," (14:34–35). Recognizing that the women instructed in corporate worship practices were married women in that context may indicate that these same women were the ones instructed in corporate worship practices in chapter 11. This observation does not insist that chapter 14 is the precedent for chapter 11 (see more discussion on this approach on page 60); however, the same context is in view in both passages, making the observation relevant.

Commentary, eds. John F. Walvoord and Roy B. Zuck (Wheaton: Victor, 1983), 529, parenthetical notes original. Charles Hodge also teaches this in his commentary on 1 Corinthians.

[6] W. Harold Mare, "1 Corinthians," *The Expositor's Bible Commentary*, eds. Frank E. Gaebelein and J.D. Douglas (Grand Rapids: Zondervan, 1976), 255; Robert Gromacki, *Called to Be Saints* (The Woodlands: Kress, 2002), 134–135; Thomas R. Schreiner, *1 Corinthians* (Downers Grove: InterVarsity Press Academic, 2018), 229, 231–232.

- There are also reasons to believe that Paul was speaking about all men and women generally. Below are some reasons why a person may interpret the text that way.

  ▷ Every time Paul referred to husbands and wives in his epistles using the terms *anēr* and *gunē*, it was within a context that plainly revealed his intention (1 Corinthians 7:1–7, Ephesians 5:22–33, Colossians 3:18–19). It would be unusual for the apostle to address husbands and wives without clearly establishing that context by either mentioning marriage explicitly or using possessive terminology like "their own" in 1 Corinthians 14:35.

  ▷ As far as can be known, "praying or prophesying" (vv. 4–5) was not limited to married women in the assembly; therefore, instructions for how women appeared while functioning in these ways may not have been limited to the married participants.

  ▷ In vv. 7–10, the apostle spoke of man and woman with various combinations of definite/indefinite articles, or with no article at all. This seems to indicate a general view of all men and all women—and he was still instructing about coverings in that section (vv. 8, 10).

  ▷ In vv. 11–13, Paul broadened the scope of his view and clearly no longer referred only to the marital relationship, stating, "the man *has his birth* through the woman," (italics original). He used the singular forms of *anēr* and *gunē* (even with definite articles in

v. 12!) to speak of men and women generally, leading to another mention of women covering their heads (v. 13). This potentially indicates that he had all women in view in the rhetorical question of v. 13 and even from the start of his instruction.

▷ Paul's points about hair lengths clearly move outside of the marital relationship again in vv. 14–15, potentially indicating that the preceding instructions regarding the covering apply to people in the church more broadly.

4. Scripture testifies that God has designed a purpose for each gender's appearance.

◆ When reading through 1 Corinthians 11, some will dismiss the notion of its continued significance based on reasoning that says God is not concerned with outward appearances. First Samuel 16:7 says, "For man looks at the outward appearance, but the Lord looks at the heart," and this verse has often been abused as a proof text for such reactions. It is true that God sees the heart—He sees more deeply and truly than mere man ever could—yet, it is also true that He has a purpose for man's appearance.

◆ The Law states, "A woman shall not wear man's clothing, nor shall a man put on a woman's clothing; for whoever does these things is an abomination to the Lord your God," (Deuteronomy 22:5). God communicated a moral point to Israel: gender distinction should be communicated by externals. This principle continues today.[7]

- This moral point is rooted in the beginnings of mankind. Genesis 2–3 details the creation and fall of men and women and it is rightly understood that they were different in role, function, and appearance. Though speculative, it is a very small jump to deduce that when the Lord clothed Adam and Eve (Genesis 3:21), their clothes had distinguishing features, matching their distinguished designs.

- Although there is no spiritual advantage to being male or female (Galatians 3:28), there remains a distinction between the sexes. The New Testament embraces this distinction in its directives regarding the roles, function, and appearance of men and women (1 Timothy 2:9–15, 1 Peter 3:1–7). God has given gendered instructions regarding outward appearance to the new covenant community in more places than 1 Corinthians 11.

---

[7] Women are not limited to skirts and men need not commit themselves to beards. These are conscience decisions for individuals, not biblical directives. External gender distinctions in everyday attire are to be recognized in principle by making wise choices, not through manmade laws that seek to bind the consciences of others (a means of control) apart from the word of God.

5. **The burden of proof regarding the application of head covering and hair lengths (HCHL) in 1 Corinthians 11 falls on those who say the instructions are not applicable for the church today.**

- ◆ This point must be grasped early on in reading this passage, as it is a guiding principle of interpretation.

- ◆ It is certainly true that faithful Bible interpretation distinguishes between transcendent principles and cultural customs. However, this distinction cannot be assumed—it must always be proven. All instructions for the church in the New Testament epistles are to be received as transcendent and binding unless they can be proven to be a custom that was relevant to the original audience only.[8]

- ◆ Christians are obligated to apply the New Testament text as it is stated, and a natural reading of 1 Corinthians 11 results in the reader's obligation to obey it. There is no time-related aspect in the text that would establish an expiration for its ongoing significance for the church;

---

[8] R.C. Sproul was very direct on this point when he said, "There are times when it is not immediately apparent to determine what is principle and what is custom…The burden of proof is always on the one who says it's custom rather than principle…If I'm going to err, I'd rather err on the side of being overscrupulous of treating something that was a local custom as if it were a transcendent principle rather than ever being guilty of taking a transcultural principle of Almighty God and reducing it to a first-century custom," (Head Covering Movement, "What RC Sproul Believes About Head Covering," YouTube: https://youtu.be/X1Zmjyvet_4, Accessed August 2022).

therefore, those who claim the significance has expired must offer their reasoning. Christians should need to be convinced *out* of plain interpretation and application, not *into* it.

6. **Most believers throughout church history have not seen the instructions about HCHL as particularly difficult or controversial.**

* This point does not settle any debate over the passage in question. It does, however, give believers reason to pause when claiming the text is uniquely difficult to understand and its application dubious. In previous generations, this passage was largely uncontroversial and plainly applied.

* By and large, the church, across different generations, cultures, and denominations has embraced the contemporary application of this passage. This sample is worth considering: Clement of Alexandria, Tertullian, Augustine, Thomas Aquinas, William Tyndale, Desiderius Erasmus, Martin Luther, John Calvin,[9] John

---

[9] Calvin felt so strongly about this that he said, "So if women are thus permitted to have their heads uncovered and to show their hair, they will eventually be allowed to expose their entire breasts, and they will come to make their exhibitions as if it were a tavern show; they will become so brazen that modesty and shame will be no more; in short, they will forget the duty of nature," from *Men, Women and Order in the Church: Three Sermons by John Calvin* (Dallas: Presbyterian Heritage Publications, 1992), 12–13.

Bunyan, John Gill, John Wesley, Charles Spurgeon, H.A. Ironside, A.W. Pink, Martyn Lloyd-Jones, S. Lewis Johnson, C.K. Barrett, Charles Ryrie, Bruce Waltke, and R.C. Sproul.[10] These all taught that HCHL instructions are transcendent instructions that are to be observed in the church without exception. Given the wide range of their individual beliefs on Bible doctrines, this is certainly one of the very few non-gospel doctrines they all agreed on!

7. **This passage speaks to both sexes and provides HCHL instruction for each.**

- ◆ It is disingenuous to approach the text with just one gender in mind. (e.g., "This passage is about women covering their heads," or, "This passage is about men not having long hair.") First Timothy 2:9–15 is an example of a passage that instructs only one gender, though it is not without complementarity (note how the passage starts with "Likewise," connecting it with the verses that precede it.) First Corinthians 11:2–16 instructs both genders at the same time with an inverted symmetry— what is good for men to do is not good for women to do, and vice versa.

- ◆ It may be deduced that all men are in view in this passage, but only *married* women are in view (see "Personal Application of the Interpretation" on page 76). Although

---

[10] For a list of quotes from these men, refer to Appendix C.

this is technically a disparity, it is does not change the reality that the passage speaks to both men and women in a symmetrical way, addressing the roles of each gender.

- If maintained, the inverted symmetry presented in this passage rules out many erroneous views and will keep the reader from making inconsistent applications (see #11 below). It is difficult to overstate this point.

8. **"Traditions" in v. 2 references handed-down teachings meant to continue on as given.**

- Apostolic instruction carries full divine weight for the church. The word for "traditions" could be translated "ordinances," as in the KJV. Paul was not presenting his instructions merely as optional suggestions for the church.

- The apostle referred to all the other churches he knew of (notice his sweeping phrase in v. 16: "the churches *of God*"), stating that each of them followed his instructions on HCHL. When traditions/ordinances were presented to the church, they were expected to maintain them with the rest of the churches—with no exceptions (cf. 2 Thessalonians 2:15, 3:6). Just because an instruction is given regarding a "tradition," "custom," or "practice," that does not automatically mean there is an expiration date on the instruction.

- Steven Wedgeworth has identified the head covering custom as "lost," leading him to claim that churches could do more harm than good if they try to resurrect the practice.[11] However, one must wonder how this particular custom could be considered "lost" when it has been preserved in Scripture along with the theological foundation of the practice.

9. Covering instructions only apply to specified times.

- Paul's instructions about covering or uncovering are clearly designated for times of "praying and prophesying." Whether this activity is limited to the local church gathering will be explored in "Personal Application of the Interpretation" below. Regardless, Paul's emphasis seemed to be on the action of covering or uncovering, as opposed to some sort of uniform for men and women, like many Amish and Mennonite communities have made it out to be. The text nowhere

---

[11] Wedgeworth writes: "Customs vary according to time and place, and take their meaning from broader public interpretation… I don't believe that churches have to resurrect the custom of head coverings. Were the custom still dominant, it would be pious to respect and retain it, but a lost custom is somewhat different. When a custom is lost, the public meaning of that custom changes, and enforcing it anew can send a new and different (and, yes, mistaken) meaning," (Steven Wedgeworth, "Going on a Bear Hunt: Head Coverings, Custom, and Proper Decorum," The Gospel Coalition, https://www.thegospelcoalition.org/article/head-coverings-1-corinthians-11, Written February 24, 2021, Accessed October 2022.) For a response to "public meaning," see point #13 below.

indicates or implies 24/7 applicability for covering or uncovering the head, as though he were issuing men and women a constant-use outfit.

10. The covering instruction was given to illustrate headship, not just outward gender distinctions.

- Although gender differences are in view in Paul's instruction about physical appearances (see #4 above), the apostle's teaching is not grounded there. Recognizing the foundation of Paul's instruction is critical.

- The practice of covering or uncovering teaches something about each gender's relationship to authority. This is important to recognize, as many people today seek to reduce Paul's instruction down to "men should dress like men and women should dress like women." Paul was concerned that a symbol of *authority* was maintained (v. 10), not a symbol of femininity. Nowhere in this passage did the apostle teach distinction in appearance merely for appearance's sake. The Law may have presented the issue this way (Deuteronomy 22:5), but Paul did not.

- In v. 7, Paul explained why it is disgraceful for a man to cover his head while praying or prophesying: It is because man "is the image and glory of God." The same verse goes on to say that woman, by contrast, "is the glory of man." Therefore, the covering (or lack thereof) does not just identify men as males and women as females; it is intended to communicate the person's relationship to another's authority.

▷ Scripture is clear that man and woman both bear the image of God (Genesis 1:26–27, 5:1–2, Mark 10:6). The apostle was not denying women the image of God by stating "[man] is the image and glory of God," while saying "woman is the glory of man," without reference to her bearing God's image. Rather, Paul was emphasizing the relationship each gender has to the glory of another. Man is the image and glory of God; woman is not man's image, but she is his glory.

▷ Man was created first from the dust of the ground, and, from his beginning, was to serve God by stewarding the earth (Genesis 1:26, 2:7–9, 15). Conversely, woman has her origin in man—as opposed to dust—and, from her beginning, was to serve God by helping man steward the earth (Genesis 2:18–25, 1 Corinthians 11:8–9). Paul's reasoning here is consistent with his reasoning in 1 Timothy 2, where he stated that women are not to teach or have authority over men in the church because woman was not created first (vv. 9–15).

▷ There is debate as to whether the apostle was speaking of woman as she is by nature or woman in her role as wife in vv. 7b–10. Some take the position that women are not naturally the glory of man, but *become* the glory of man through marriage, putting themselves

into a similar position as Eve, the help-mate and wife of a man. Others believe that all women are the glory of man by default.

- Proponents of the "married women" view of that passage might argue that Paul's clear reference to the Genesis 1–2 narrative in vv. 7–10 indicates he was instructing women who are married, like Eve, who was created "for the man's sake," (v. 9). In this interpretation, it is understood that the covering only represents submission to her husband as her "head" (vv. 3, 10). Seemingly taking this view, David Garland has written, "Paul reasons that a woman must cover her anatomical head, which reflects man's glory, who is her metaphorical head. If a woman were to appear in worship with her head uncovered, the splendor of her tresses (11:15) would bring honor to *her husband* when all ought to be concerned with glorifying God alone," (emphasis added).[12]

- Proponents of the "all women" view of that passage could point out that Paul did not seem to establish the context of the marital relationship in the text, particularly as he continued his reasoning into v. 12. In this interpretation, it is understood that the

---

[12] David E. Garland, *1 Corinthians* (Grand Rapids: Baker Academic, 2003), 523.

covering represents more than the role of a wife only. Instead, the covering would represent women's created nature to be in helpers of man generally, following and assisting men, whom God has designated to lead. It is difficult to find commentators who teach this explicitly.

▷ Regardless of which particular women are in view, the text indicates that the relationship these women have to men is one of submission—yielding to the authoritative head. Paul concluded his thought about woman being the glory of man by stating, "Therefore the woman ought to have *a symbol of* authority on her head," (v. 10, italics original). Woman's role as the glory of man necessarily includes submission to man, and this is the basis of the covering instruction as opposed to mere gender distinction.

11. The woman's covering described in vv. 5-6, 10 is not her hair.

◆ Those who believe the covering of vv. 5-6, 10 is a woman's hair base their reasoning off v. 15 which states, "Her hair is given to her as a covering."[13]

---

[13] GotQuestions.org takes this position, stating "This covering [of 1 Corinthians 11:5-6] not only means a cloth but also can refer to a woman's hair length... The Apostle Paul is saying here that in the Corinthian culture, when a wife's hair was longer than her husband's, it showed her submission to his headship," ("Should Christian women wear head coverings?", Got

> Most advocates of this view state that a woman's long hair is the definition of the covering in vv. 5–6.[14] Some who hold this view believe that Paul was instructing women to keep their hair long enough to be able put it up on their head when praying and prophesying.[15]

♦ There are three main reasons why this view fails.

> If hair defines the covering of v. 4, men would be required to have shaved heads because it would be inappropriate for them to ever pray or prophesy in the gathered assembly with hair on their heads. If it was improper for men to pray *uncovered* and hair is the *covering*, then men must be bald in order to pray properly.

> If hair is the covering of v. 6, Paul's instructions would become impossible to understand. The text would essentially state this: "For if a woman has short hair or a shaved head, let her also have her hair cut off or her

Questions, https://www.gotquestions.org/head-coverings.html, Accessed August 2022).

[14] J.B. Hurley articulates this in the form of a hypothetical question in his book *Man and Woman in Biblical Perspective*: "Could it be that Paul was not asking the Corinthian women to put on veils, but was asking them to continue wearing their hair in the distinctive fashion of women?" (Grand Rapids: Zondervan, 1981), 170–171.

[15] Sam Waldron holds this view, stating, "The covering is long hair done up (or styled) in an orderly or tidy fashion," as cited by Brandon Adams, who summarizes and explains this view in "Watch Your Head," Contrast, https://contrast2.wordpress.com/2009/07/16/watch-your-head, Accessed October 2022.

head shaved." If her hair was already cut short, he would not have to say that she should go on to cut her hair short. If her head was already shaved, he would not have to say that she should go on to shave her head.

▷ The "covering" of v. 15 is an entirely different Greek word than the word used to refer to covering in vv. 5–6.[16] Additionally, vv. 4–6 reference Christians in worship, whereas vv. 14–15 reference all people everywhere. These distinctions in context must be seriously considered when seeking to define the covering of vv. 4–6 by the covering of v. 15. It is difficult to see how this interpretation stands amid these challenges.

12. Instructions about gender roles and HCHL stand or fall together in this passage because they share the same foundation: God's created design.

◆ The basis for covering/uncovering is the authority structure found in God's design (v. 10). Recognizing this design is essential to upholding the doctrine of biblical complementarianism. Eve's submission to Adam was germane to her role from the day she was created.

---

[16] The dominant word for covering/uncovering in the passage is the verb *katakaluptó* (vv. 5, 6, 7, 13), meaning simply to veil or cover the head. The word in v. 15 is the noun *peribolaion* and it refers to an article of clothing like a robe.

- If the man covers his head while praying or prophesying, he is in conflict with his God-given role. If the woman uncovers her head while praying or prophesying, she is in conflict with her God-given role.

  ▷ Man shames Christ if his head is covered *because* Christ is his authority (v. 4). Man ought not cover *because* he is the glory of God (v. 7a). The foundation of Paul's reasoning is God's created design for authority structure.

  ▷ Woman shames man if her head is uncovered *because* man is her authority (v. 5). A woman ought to cover *because* she is the glory of man (v. 7b). Again, the foundation of Paul's reasoning is God's created design for authority structure.

  ▷ The distinction in authority is the basis for Paul's instruction in these verses. Paul argued that if his instructions are dismissed, the roles themselves are infringed upon. The Corinthians were expected to both recognize his reasoning *and* embrace his instruction because they are inseparable in the letter. Uncovering and covering during prayer and prophecy are instructed *based on* God's created design for men's and women's complementary roles.

- If a woman uncovers her head during prayer and prophecy, she renders herself *the same as* the unnatural woman whose hair is cut short or shaved.

▷ To understand the potency of Paul's argument here, vv. 14–15 should be considered. At that point in the passage, Paul described God's design for hair by citing God as the Giver of a natural covering for women. He also stated that mankind, by instinct, recognizes that women should embrace the natural covering, and that for men to imitate it by growing their hair out is shameful. Thus, in v. 6, Paul was saying that just as any woman's shaved head is unnatural and shameful, *so is* a Christian woman's uncovered head during prayer and prophecy.

▷ Paul's argument is that if a woman refuses to wear a covering on her head during prayer and prophecy, she is refusing her role as a woman and may as well reject God's natural covering by cutting her hair short or shaving her head. This means that the basis for Paul's instructions on hair lengths is also rooted in God's design—just like the head covering and gender roles themselves.

◆ The points are all connected. To isolate the application of Paul's instruction from the foundation of his reasoning is to divide, and therefore nullify, the teaching altogether. It would be inconsistent to claim the continuing significance of hair lengths instruction while rejecting the covering instructions—and there is no exegetical basis for it.

13. Gender roles and HCHL were not cultural instructions.

♦ Although all of Scripture was written in cultural contexts, no Scripture was ever breathed out by the culture. The Bible was inspired by God alone and Paul's instructions were given to the church from God, not the culture. It is worth noting that in the passage Paul did not mention the cultures of Corinth, the greater Greco-Roman world, or any other place. He appealed to the created design, nature itself, and angels as the basis for his instruction, and each of those points transcends any given culture in the global church. There is no exegetical argument that Paul's instructions were cultural in any sense. This point alone should be enough for Christians to accept the ongoing observance of the apostle's instruction; nevertheless, many Christians demand more evidence.

♦ "Nature" (as opposed to culture) in v. 14 references how things are and should be, according to God's design.

  ▷ The word for "nature" here is φύσις (*physis*), meaning "essence, native condition, native instinct."[17]

---

[17] W.D. Mounce, *Mounce's Complete Expository Dictionary of Old & New Testament Words* (Grand Rapids: Zondervan, 2006), 1307–1308. Paul's other usages of the word in its various forms can be found in Romans 1:26–27, 2:14, 27, 11:21, 24, 1 Corinthians 11:14, Galatians 2:15, 4:8, and Ephesians 2:3. The word also appears in James 3:7, 2 Peter 1:4, 2:12, and Jude 10. Each of these uses refers to the way things are in accordance with God's design.

▷ According to the *Theological Dictionary of the New Testament*[18] and the *Vocabulary of the Greek New Testament*,[19] the uses of *physis* in the extrabiblical contemporary writings are entirely consistent with Paul's usage with reference to native condition or instinct. In its semantic range, the word never refers to temporary cultural conditions, expectations, or expressions; thus, it is intellectually dishonest to interpret *physis* as some sort of fad or fashion by relating it to the supposed cultural norms of the day.

▷ "Disgraceful" in v. 6 refers to vileness and indecency. It is extremely unlikely that Paul would use such a strong word if he was merely referencing a temporary or optional cultural expectation of physical appearance.

♦ "Because of the angels" in v. 10 is an infamously difficult phrase to interpret. However, at a minimum, it can be said that this foundation for the apostle's reasoning transcends culture, since angels are active in and relate to the church throughout all ages. Charles Spurgeon said, "The apostle says that a woman is to have a covering upon her head because of the angels, since the angels are present in the assembly and they mark every act of indecorum, and therefore everything is to be conducted

---

[18] G. Kittle and G. Friedrich, eds., *Theological Dictionary of the New Testament*, Volume IX (Grand Rapids: Eerdmans, 1974), 251ff.

[19] J.H. Moulton and G. Milligan, *Vocabulary of the Greek New Testament* (Peabody: Hendrickson, 2004), 679.

with decency and order in the presence of the angelic spirits."[20]

- Essential to the "cultural interpretation" is the understanding that Paul wanted the Corinthians to pay attention to their surrounding culture's practices in pagan worship, customs, or immoral practices, and behave reactively. For instance, Bruce Winter boldly asserts, "What does it mean for a wife or woman to cover her head? What did that communicate in the Greco-Roman culture of Paul's day? If you can't answer those questions, then I don't think you can accurately understand this passage."[21] However, nowhere in this passage did Paul ground his instruction to believers in the culture. It could be said that it would actually go against the apostle's track record found in his epistles to base his instruction for worship practices on the world (cf. Romans 12:1-2).

  ▷ It is critical to realize that there is no monolithic form of the cultural argument and there are rarely solid historical citations for sweeping statements about the general understanding of the cultures of that time. In fact, it would be difficult to know exactly which

---

[20] C.H. Spurgeon, *The Metropolitan Tabernacle Pulpit* (London: Passmore and Alabaster, 1863), 263.

[21] Bruce Winter, "The Appearance of Unveiled Wives in 1 Corinthians 11:2-16," in *Roman Wives, Roman Widows: The Appearance of New Women and the Pauline Communities* (Grand Rapids: Eerdmans, 2003), 77-96.

subculture of that time to single out and examine in such a study (Hellenistic, Athenian, Spartan, Patrician, Plebeian, etc.).

▷ Some proponents of the cultural view state that Paul's instruction was for the Corinthians to *imitate* the surrounding culture.[22] Other proponents state that Paul wanted the Corinthians to *do the opposite* of what their culture was doing.[23] Some do not make a claim

---

[22] Many teachers will make dubious general claims at this point, as BibleRef.com has done: "Apparently, nearly all women wore head coverings in public during this era," ("What does 1 Corinthians chapter 11 mean?", BibleRef, https://www.bibleref.com/1-Corinthians/11/1-Corinthians-chapter-11.html, Accessed August 2022). The conclusion here is that Paul's argument is rooted in a unanimous cultural custom, but there is no evidence of this. Further, this author has found no evidence of covering being practiced for the purpose of *illustrating authority structure* within the culture (see point #10 above).

[23] Albert Barnes commented, "It would seem from this that the women removed their veils, and wore their hair disheveled, when they pretended to be under the influence of divine inspiration. This was the case with the pagan priestesses; and in so doing, the Christian women imitated them. On this account, if on no other, Paul declares the impropriety of this conduct," (quote found under *Barnes' Notes on The Bible* for 1 Corinthians 11:5 at https://biblehub.com/commentaries/1_corinthians/11-5.htm, Accessed August 2022). Some commentators will assert that pagan men in the culture would cover their heads while praying to their pagan gods and that was Paul's basis for telling Christian men to be uncovered. Other commentators assert that when women uncovered their heads, they were stating that they were "available" to potential male suitors (see David Garland's *1 Corinthians* in the Baker Exegetical Commentary series, p. 521). No commentator has furnished a convincing body of evidence on any of these claims.

one way or another, but still insist that it must have been cultural in some form or fashion.[24] There are obvious issues with such views.

- If Paul was encouraging the Corinthians to mimic the common worship practices of their culture, he was actually encouraging them to copy the practices of demon-worshipers (cf. 1 Corinthians 10:20).

- According to Paul in v. 16, it was the custom of all the churches he knew of—from Jerusalem to Macedonia to Rome—to have the women cover and the men uncover during prayer and prophecy. This means that the practice transcended any customs local to the Corinthians.

◆ It cannot be assumed that the covering was cultural because there is no convincing evidence to say Corinth's culture generally viewed HCHL any one way.

▷ Cultural views and practices regarding **hair lengths** varied by subculture.

- Some say that Paul's describing a woman's shaved head as "disgraceful" was founded upon a scenario in Corinth where the prostitutes would shave their

---

[24] See John MacArthur's rather abrupt statement at the end of his commentary on this passage, in which he states that women were only to cover "where custom dictated it," without providing any citations or further explanation in *First Corinthians* (Chicago: Moody, 1984), 263.

heads as a sign of their lewdness.[25] This interpretation obviously does not come from the text, but what is more interesting is that it also does not come from any meaningful historical research. It should be considered a hypothesis at best.[26]

- There is good evidence to suggest that some adulterous women would have their hair cut short by their husbands when they were found out.[27] This was done to publicly shame them, because long hair is natural for women. However, Plutarch reported that in Greece women would willingly cut their hair off (and men would let theirs grow out) for good luck against misfortunes in life.[28]

---

[25] See James Burton Coffman, "Commentary on 1 Corinthians 11," *Coffman Commentaries on the Old and New Testament* (Abilene: Abilene Christian University Press, 1974). Available online at https://www.studylight.org /commentaries/eng/bcc/1-corinthians-11.html, Accessed August 2022. Many who take this position also say that a woman's uncovered head also indicated sexual promiscuity, but archaeological discoveries do not back this claim. For an example of Greek pottery from Paul's time period featuring a nude mistress with both hair *and* a headdress, see "Image of St. Petersburg 644," Perseus Digital Library, http://www.perseus.tufts.edu /hopper/image?img=Perseus:image:1993.01.0366, Accessed August 2022.

[26] Gordon Fee summarized this theory well: "It seems to be a case of one scholar's guess becoming a second scholar's footnote and a third scholar's assumption," (*Corinthians*, 563 n. 84).

[27] This description is found in Dio Chrysostom's *Speeches*: "A woman guilty of adultery shall have her hair cut off and be a harlot," (64.3). Dio Chrysostom lived from about 40–115 AD.

[28] Plutarch, *Moralia*, The Roman Questions 14. Plutarch lived from 46 to about 119 AD.

- In the Greco-Roman world, Spartan men would let their hair grow long after puberty and both men and women were known for tying their hair in a knot over the crowns of their heads.[29] Athenian men, on the other hand, would cut their hair short upon puberty and the cutting of the hair was in itself a religious ceremony. Athenian women would often be found in headdresses.[30]

- Generally speaking, Jewish men kept their hair short and Jewish women kept theirs long.[31] Jewish men who were under the Nazarite vow were not allowed to cut their hair (Numbers 6:1–21).[32]

---

[29] Anna Wichmann, "Why Spartan Men Had Long Hair," Greek Reporter, https://greekreporter.com/2022/02/20/spartan-men-long-hair-ancient-greece, Accessed August 2022.

[30] An entry from *A Dictionary of Greek and Roman Antiquities* about Greek hair (online transcription created by Bill Thayer) is quite informative regarding both men and women in Sparta and Athens. This fantastic entry on κόμη (Gr. "hair") provides many helpful references and citations: William Smith, D.C.L., LL.D., ed., *A Dictionary of Greek and Roman Antiquities* (London: John Murray, 1875), 328–330, as cited in "Coma," Bill Thayer's Web Site, https://penelope.uchicago.edu/Thayer/E/Roman/Texts/secondary/SMIGRA*/Coma.html, Accessed August 2022.

[31] Ibid.

[32] This was one of several unnatural acts contained within the vow. The Nazirite vow is addressed in more detail in the next section, "Answering Various Objections."

- Thus, there is no convincing evidence to say Corinth's culture generally viewed hair lengths any one way.

▷ Cultural views and practices regarding **coverings** also varied by subculture.

- Gentile men would not veil their heads in everyday life, but many of them veiled their heads as a custom in worship. Virgil, Dionysius, and Plutarch all noted this practice around the time of Christ.[33] Richard Oster notes, "The practice of men covering their heads in the context of prayer and prophecy was a common pattern of Roman piety and widespread during the late Republic and early Empire. Since Corinth was a Roman colony, there should be little doubt that this aspect of Roman religious practice deserves greater attention by commentators than it has received."[34]

- Covering practices for Gentile women varied greatly. Some, like the Athenians, wore bands and silk nets frequently in everyday life.[35] Spartan

---

[33] Virgil, *Aeneis*, 3.403–409, Dionysius of Halicarnassus, *The Roman Antiquities*, 12.16.4, and Plutarch, *Moralia*, The Romans Questions 10. Virgil lived from about 70–19 BC and Dionysisus lived from about 60–7 BC.

[34] Richard E. Oster, Jr., "Use, Misuse, and Neglect of Archaeological Evidence in Some Modern Works on 1 Corinthians," *Zeitschrift für die Neutestamentliche Wissenschaft*, vol. 83 (1992), 52–73.

[35] Smith, *A Dictionary of Greek and Roman Antiquities*.

women regularly covered, too.[36] Other women were often uncovered, as research into the Greco-Roman culture has revealed.[37] There was no broad or consistent cultural understanding that a woman's covering or uncovering in everyday life indicated anything in particular.

- The Jewish custom of that day was for women to cover their hair with some sort of band or veil any time they left the house, which most certainly included corporate worship settings.[38]

- Jewish men had a garment they used to cover themselves to protect them from environmental elements and to remind them of God's calling on their lives (Numbers 15:37–40, Deuteronomy 22:12). God never instructed Jewish men to cover themselves with this garment during prayer, but cultural studies show that this use of the garment became a popular custom. Eventually, Jewish men

---

[36] Plutarch, *Moralia*, Sayings of Spartans, Charillus 2.

[37] See Verena Zinserling's book *Women in Greece and Rome* (Montclair: Abner Schram, 1973). Helpful online resources include "Pictures of Women on Greek Vases from the Perseus Web Site," BTerry.com, https://www.bterry.com/1cor/vases.htm, and Michael Marlowe's "Headcovering Customs of the Ancient World: An Illustrated Survey," Bible Research, https://www.bible-researcher.com/headcoverings3.html, Both websites accessed August 2022.

[38] Rabbi Mayer Schiller, "The Obligation of Married Women to Cover Their Hair," *The Journal of Halacha* (1985), 81–108.

began wearing tallits and kippahs (or "yarmulke," pronounced *yah-ma-kah*) in everyday life.[39]

- There is no convincing body of evidence that any of these cultural sub-groups used coverings as illustrations of authority/headship. Despite this fact, Wayne Grudem has asserted about the general culture: "Head coverings in the first century were a sign of relation to authority."[40] This is an unwise statement. The culture did not have a unified, widespread reason for covering. Gordon Fee rightly responded to Grudem: "Since the evidence is so ambiguous, both for the wearing of head coverings and the reasons for it, one would need to demonstrate such a universal statement with hard evidence."[41] Such hard evidence simply does not exist.

  - Thus, there is no convincing evidence to say Corinth's culture generally viewed head coverings any one way.

- It cannot be assumed that the covering was cultural because culture does not always determine physical expressions in the church.

---

[39] See Maimonides' description of this Jewish practice in the 12th Century quoted by Richard C.H. Lenski in *The Interpretation of St. Paul's First and Second Epistle to the Corinthians* (Fortress Press, 1946), 435.

[40] Grudem, "Κεφαλή," 56.

[41] Fee, *Corinthians*, 556 n. 47.

▷ Although the corporate worship of the local body transcends culture, there are some elements in the worship service that have always been culturally conditioned. Technologies, instrumentation, and even interpersonal greetings all vary from generation to generation and are dependent on a variety of factors. The HCHL instruction, however, is not presented as a culturally-conditioned aspect of the gathering in this text. The instruction is backed by transcendent principles that apply in all generations.

▷ Using the culture as a litmus test for determining the validity of a physical expression of worship is often unwise. Traditionally, the Salvation Army has not observed baptism or communion, as they have asserted that those symbols are not recognized by today's culture, rendering them obsolete.[42] They teach that the swearing-in of one of their members under the Army's flag acknowledges the same beliefs that

---

[42] The Salvation Army has not released many official statements on the sacraments/ordinances that are accessible today. However, at least two international Salvation Army outposts have made such statements. See "Why does The Salvation Army not baptise (sic) or hold communion?", Waterbeach & Soham Salvation Army Community Church, https://web.archive.org/web/20160304042657/http://www.waterbeachsalvationarmy.org.uk/what-to-know-more/why-does-the-salvation-army-not-baptise-or-hold-communion, and "Our Beliefs," The Salvation Army, India, https://www.salvationarmy.org/india/ourbeliefs, Both websites accessed August 2022.

first-century water baptism communicated, and that "there are many worthy ways of publicly witnessing to having been baptized into Christ's body."[43] The vast majority of Christendom rejects this approach to church ordinances based on Scripture's indication that these physical expressions are actually transcendent customs meant for all generations.

▷ As noted, it is particularly important to the conversation about HCHL that the physical expression is meant to illustrate headship, not just outward gender distinctions (see #10 above). Paul even gave a specific location for the symbol (vv. 4–6, 10); the physical head is to be used to teach something about the figurative head. Bible readers who seek to make the apostle's instructions purely cultural must consider what, if anything, from their current culture would be used to illustrate the enduring principle of headship in the corporate worship setting.[44] To be consistent with their own interpretation in their application, the symbol should involve the head, not

---

[43] Ibid.

[44] Far too often the symbolism that Paul instructs is quickly dismissed. For instance, in writing for *The Gospel Coalition*, Benjamin L. Merkle states, "[A head covering] had no meaning in itself, but was a concrete expression of an intangible truth. Thus, Paul isn't concerned with head coverings *per se*. Rather, he's concerned with the meaning that wearing a head covering conveys," ("Should Women Wear Head Coverings?", The Gospel Coalition, https://www.thegospelcoalition.org/article/should-women-wear-head-coverings, Accessed August 2022).

be worn by men when it is worn by women, and be well-understood by the non-Christian community.[45] In any case, it seems that far too often in dismissing the practice, those who hold to this view of the custom also dismiss the principle of symbolizing headship while in fellowship.[46] This is inevitable because the

---

[45] It would have to be well-understood by the non-Christian community because if the practice was taken from the culture either to be copied or rejected, non-believing people attending the fellowship (cf. 1 Cor 14:23) would have understood what the Christians were conveying in their symbolism. If Paul was instructing believers to borrow from their culture to symbolize these spiritual principles throughout the ages, believers today would need to take something from their cultures that unbelievers would recognize if they were to walk into the gathered assembly.

[46] In a sermon preached in 2007, the now-apostate Joshua Harris said, "Covering the head for the woman was the common symbol of being married, of being someone's wife. In some ways it's not unlike our cultural practice of wearing a wedding ring. It was a visual symbol that would very quickly allow someone to identify you as a married person, as a married woman. It was a statement that you belonged to your husband." (Although the sermon has been removed from the church website, it can still be accessed through the *Wayback Machine* here: https://web.archive.org/web /20071005131818/http://www.covlife.org/sermons/streambox.php?title= Men,%20Women%20and%20Headgear&speaker=Joshua%20Harris&day name=Sunday&month=September&day=4&year=2007&path=http://covli femedia.org/sunday_am/2007_09_02%201%20Corinthians%20Part%2023 %20-%20Harris&movsize=12.2, Accessed December 2022.) Daniel Wallace claims that modest clothing is a better modern replacement for a woman's covering ("What is the Head Covering in 1 Cor 11:2-16 and Does it Apply to Us Today?", Bible.org, https://bible.org/article/what-head-covering-1- cor-112-16-and-does-it-apply-us-today, Accessed August 2022). The recommendations set forth by Harris and Wallace do nothing to illustrate

points are all connected (see #12 above). The principle is not mere existence of male headship, but also *symbolizing* male headship in the gathered assembly.

▷ Finally, as one considers whether the culture determines this physical expression in the church, the question must be asked: If this teaching is rooted in the culture, what should happen if a culture utterly rejects the notion of headship altogether? Many cultures today have done this very thing and it seems quite illogical to think that Paul would instruct churches today to just "go with the culture." If a culture rejects the concept of male headship and, naturally, all physical expressions of that headship, Scripture must still be upheld.

- The practice of covering was not merely cultural because it extended beyond Corinth.

    ▷ The apostles instructed all the churches to observe these same instructions about HCHL (v. 16, note how Paul said, "we"). All the churches of which Paul was aware were following his instructions on HCHL.

    ▷ Apparently, Paul anticipated some members of the church in Corinth to be uniquely stubborn in this matter, as they were in other matters (cf. 1:11, 4:14,

---

headship in today's cultures, nor do they maintain the inverted symmetry of the instruction. For those who desire to change out the symbol for something that a non-Christian culture understands more readily, the symbol must still reflect the teaching of authority and headship. This, of course, is a near-impossible task in many places today.

5:1–2, 11:17–18), yet he never presented the practice as a "doubtful thing" to be left to individual consciences (cf. Romans 14:1). Instead, the apostle issued a closing statement on this topic that informed the Corinthians that if they rejected his teaching on HCHL, they would be the only church doing so.

- A very important factor that is often overlooked is that if the gathered Christian assembly is in view, and not the Christian witness to the culture in everyday life, it would be illogical for Paul to base his instructions on the culture. Regardless of what the culture was doing, the instructions of 1 Corinthians 11 would refer to the church gathered in corporate worship. The very nature of this scene is transcendent across cultures because Jesus Christ has built His church across cultures. As God's people gathered for worship, they were not witnessing to the culture with their HCHL; they were worshiping God and displaying truth for the angels. If Paul had outsiders in mind, he would have mentioned it as he did in 14:23.

Answering Various Objections

Several objections to the continuing application of HCHL from 1 Corinthians 11 naturally arise, and some of the objections are strong. The most common retorts are listed below, paired with biblical responses.

Why did Paul tell the Corinthians to judge for themselves (v. 13) if the practice is not optional?

When Paul urged the Corinthians to employ their own discernment on this issue, he was not offering them an opportunity to disagree with him; this issue was not to be settled by personal opinion. Earlier in this same letter, Paul encouraged the church to agree with him in their collective judgment regarding communion when he wrote, "I speak as to wise men; *you judge* what I say," (10:15, emphasis added) before going on to ask them rhetorical questions. In the same way, he expected them to fully understand and embrace his instruction regarding HCHL.

Paul was no stranger to the practice of making his audience "the judge," intending them answering his rhetorical questions in a certain way. Readers do well to consider Paul's powerful use of rhetorical questions in Romans 8:31–35, and the questions he posed to the churches of Galatia in Galatians 3:3, 4:15–16, and 21. In none of these instances did the apostle encourage or expect his readers to disagree with him.

Further, Paul's question incorporates the word "proper" (Gr. πρέπω), as he asked, "Judge for yourselves: is it proper for a woman to pray to God *with her head* uncovered?" (italics original). The word for "proper" makes reference to the fitness or appropriateness of a certain action in accordance with sound doctrine (Ephesians 5:3, Titus 2:1). This rhetorical question highlights the *theological significance* of a woman's covering her head during prayer, as opposed to some sort of cultural expectation. The other New Testament uses of this word consistently appeal to sound doctrine, not cultural conformity (Matthew 3:15, 1 Timothy 2:10, Hebrews 2:10, 7:26).

Finally, it should also be noticed that Paul incorporated an imperative into his HCHL instruction. Aside from the command to "judge for yourselves" in v. 13, the only imperative in the passage is found in v. 6 when the apostle wrote, "if it is disgraceful for a woman to have her hair cut off or her head shaved, *let her cover* her head," (imperative italicized). Paul was expressing that a woman who does not have long hair is obviously unnatural, and her desire to be in that state is plainly disgraceful. "If this really is the case," he essentially said, "women should (imperative) cover their heads."[1] Paul was not presenting the covering as an option to be personally accepted or rejected.

Why did Paul say, "we have no such practice" (v. 16)?

The translation and interpretation of the apostle's phrasing here has been the subject of some disagreement. The ESV translation is found in the question above. The NIV renders it, "we have no other practice," while the KJV replaces "practice" with "custom." The NLT is phrased, "we have no other custom than this."

Thomas Schreiner rightly handles this phrase in offering this commentary:

> Now, some have said that Paul actually rejects the wearing of head coverings by women with these words because the Greek literally says, 'we have no *such practice*,' and thus they conclude that the practice of wearing head coverings is renounced here by Paul. But such an understanding is surely wrong. Paul in this verse is addressing the contentious, who, the previous context makes clear, *do not want to wear a head covering*. The practice of certain Corinthian women who *refuse to wear a head covering* is what Paul refers to when he says, 'we have no such

---

[1] "Should" language, reflecting the imperative nature of the Greek, is incorporated in some English translations of v. 6, including the NIV, NLT, NET, and HCSB (though not in its updated version, the CSB). The NASB2020 reads, "*have* her cover her head," (emphasis added).

practice.' Thus, he says to the contentious that both the apostolic circle ('we') and the rest of the churches adhere to the custom of head coverings.[2] (italics original)

To understand what Paul was communicating from a different angle, Zac Poonen has made an interesting remark on this portion of the passage:

The Holy Spirit recognized that twenty centuries later this would become a controversial issue; and so He made Paul to state (in this same verse) that if anyone was going to be argumentative about this matter, he would not argue with such a person. He would just allow that person to continue on in his/her disobedience and inconsistency.[3]

Is it reasonable to base a corporate worship practice off one passage only?

It is true that instruction concerning HCHL is only found in 1 Corinthians. This fact has created some discomfort among those considering its contemporary relevance. For instance, Steven Lawson has said:

Ideally, in interpreting the Bible we would love to see three things. We would love to see it taught by Jesus,

---

[2] Thomas Schreiner, "Head Coverings, Prophecies, and The Trinity" in *Recovering Biblical Manhood and Womanhood*, eds. John Piper and Wayne Grudem (Wheaton: Crossway, 1991), 128.

[3] "Head-Covering for Women - Zac Poonen," Sean Scott's Blog, https://preachingjesus.wordpress.com/2011/09/29/head-covering-for-women-zac-poonen, Accessed October 2022.

practiced in the book of Acts, and clarified in the epistles...Regarding head-covering, Jesus never taught this. The book of Acts gives no indication of any church in any place ever practicing this, and no other epistle beyond this one place addresses this. That is problematic.[4]

In Lawson's reasoning, a preferred presentation of a doctrine in Scripture (his standard for "ideal" based on "three things") became a *necessary condition* in just a few short sentences. When he states that it is "problematic" for HCHL instructions to have just one reference in the New Testament, he has made what is ideal to be a *necessary condition* for belief and practice. This issue is addressed more in Appendix B.

God is not bound to human standards when He issues instructions to His children. Man—Christian or otherwise—has no right to require that God should state something a minimum number of times or ways before he obeys. Milton Vincent highlighted this point in a sermon: "How many times does God have to teach something for it to be binding upon our consciences? Do we show God respect when we say, 'Lord, if you say it four times, then I'll take it seriously'? Or, 'Five times, then I'll take it seriously. But if You just say it one time, I'm not going to take it seriously'?"[5]

---

[4] Rose Michels, "STEVE LAWSON on Head Coverings," YouTube: https://youtu.be/lz0Hl-vqcPQ, Accessed August 2022.

[5] Milton Vincent, "Head Coverings in Worship pt.8," Cornerstone Fellowship Bible Church, https://www.cornerstonebible.org/series/head-coverings, Accessed August 2022. In that message, he also highlighted how

In responding to this objection, there is at least one other factor to consider. In v. 16, the apostle says that the other apostles ("we") and all the "churches of God" also embraced this instruction (cf. 1 Corinthians 1:2, 1 Thessalonians 2:14, 2 Thessalonians 1:4). This means that although the HCHL instruction is limited to one church in the preserved text, the practice of it certainly was not. Paul has eliminated the possibility that this practice was local to Corinth by referencing the other apostles and churches. It can be fairly concluded that the churches in Asia and Galatia (and every other church that Paul knew) followed the HCHL instruction, and Paul taught them this with the other apostles.

If HCHL instructions are maintained, shouldn't the holy kiss be maintained as well?

Many commentators, including Thomas Schreiner, equivalate HCHL instructions with holy kiss instructions also found in the New Testament.[6] Drawing on modern readers' instinctive recognition of the holy kiss as a cultural custom, many preachers will seek to apply the same instinct to the HCHL instructions. This should not be so, for at least three reasons.

Paul spoke of this issue more forcefully in his first letter to the Corinthians than he did about baptism, which is an insightful and intriguing point.

[6] "Mailbag #73: Dealing with Cultural Commands in 1 Corinthians 11 . . . Must All Elders Be Teachers?", 9Marks, https://www.9marks.org/mailbag/mailbag-73-dealing-with-cultural-commands-in-1-corinthians-11-must-all-elders-be-teachers, Accessed August 2022.

First, the reasoning behind holy kissing is quite different from the instructions regarding HCHL. Holy kissing is mentioned five times in the New Testament, though Peter called it a "kiss of love" (Romans 16:16, 1 Corinthians 16:20, 2 Corinthians 13:12, 1 Thessalonians 5:26, 1 Peter 5:14). Each of the five occurrences of the term is brief, with *no reasoning offered*. If the practice was reasoned to in the same way the HCHL practice was reasoned to, with an explanation of the expression's transcendent basis, it would be quite sensible to consider maintaining the practice across different cultures.

Second, holy kissing was a form of *greeting*, not a corporate worship practice. All five times the kiss appears in the New Testament, it is coupled with the word "greet." Christians were commanded to greet one another with an attitude of love; the kiss was not an aspect of their corporate worship that occurred only in the assembly. Additionally, greetings such as the holy kiss do not symbolize deep truths such as God's design for men and women, as with HCHL.

Of course, the fellowship was and continues to be of extreme importance and the many "one another" passages of the New Testament indicate that. The point remains that the holy kiss was not a physical expression that provided a symbol throughout the meeting of the assembly like the covering, nor was it a physical expression that continually communicated principles of nature like hair lengths. These distinctions should not be overlooked.

Third, the holy kiss was an *expression of acceptance* in the Christian family from *individual to individual*, whereas the

HCHL custom is a testimony of divine truth in the church to the whole body of believers, as well as to angels. The holy kiss appears as a relatively small form of interpersonal encouragement or even service. The HCHL custom, on the other hand, is a practice with deep theological significance for an entire congregation of men, women, and angels that testifies to God's created design throughout the corporate worship meeting.

If HCHL instructions are maintained, shouldn't foot-washing be maintained as well?

Many of the same voices who equivalate HCHL with holy kissing will seek the same comparison with foot-washing. The "ceremony" that takes place between Jesus and the disciples was at least partially conditioned by the culture, as their feet would have been especially disgusting due to the limited footwear of their time. Since most people see the foot-washing as a cultural custom not to be practiced with rigid imitation by the church today, does that mean the HCHL instruction of 1 Corinthians 11 should be understood in the same way? Though this comparison is interesting, there are at least three reasons why this comparison is not valid.

First, *Jesus did not teach the disciples strict imitation* of His act of love as an aspect of worship in the church. When Jesus washed the disciples' feet, He said, "If I then, the Lord and the Teacher, washed your feet, you also ought to wash one another's feet. For I gave you an example that you also should do as I did to you," (John 13:14–15). Although this may appear as a call to strict imitation, it is not.

The word for "example" in the text is *hypodeigma*, meaning "model" or something to be imitated. In Hebrews 4:11 the word is found to encourage the readers not to fall into the "same sort" of disobedience as unbelieving Israel. Those who read the letter could not fall into the *exact same* disobedience as Israel because they were not able to speak against Moses or fear the size of the Philistines (cf. Hebrews 3:16–19). Yet, it is understood that Israel provided a model of disobedience that the readers of Hebrews were still able to imitate, albeit not exactly. James 5:10 and 2 Peter 2:6 use the word the same way. If exact replication was intended, the Greek words *typos* or *mimeomai* likely would have been used instead, as in Acts 7:44, Romans 6:17, 1 Corinthians 11:1, and 2 Thessalonians 3:7–9.

Jesus' teaching during this event was focused on the principle of showing love rather than the act itself. He went on to say to His disciples, "Truly, truly, I say to you, a slave is not greater than his master, nor is one who is sent greater than the one who sent him. If you know *these things*, you are blessed if you do *them*," (vv. 16–17, emphasis added). In fact, later in the New Testament there is a possible metaphorical use of foot-washing used by Paul. When describing a true widow, the apostle said that a widow qualifies "if she has shown hospitality to strangers, if she has *washed the saints' feet*, if she has assisted those in distress," (1 Timothy 5:10, emphasis added). If this is a metaphorical phrase, it indicates that Jesus' instruction about showing sacrificial love resulted in a variety of expressions. If this is not a metaphorical phrase, it potentially reveals that there was no early church custom of washing feet in the gathered assembly because some widows did not engage in the practice.

Second, *the John 13 passage does not include any transcendent basis* for practicing foot-washing in the churches. The believers' love for one another, not the act of foot-washing itself, is based upon the transcendent love of God expressed in the Person and Work of Jesus (v. 34).

Third, *the New Testament churches were never instructed* to continue the specific act of foot-washing. Jesus did not have in view a corporate worship practice like when He taught on church discipline (cf. Matthew 18:15–18).

Does the Nazirite vow teach that men can have long hair?

In Numbers 6, God used Moses to deliver details to Israel about a special vow that could be taken by men and women alike—the vow of a Nazirite. The purpose of this vow was to be set apart for the Lord, dedicated to Him alone in a special way for a period of time. While under the vow, the vow-takers were not allowed to drink wine, strong drink, or grape juice. They were not allowed to eat fresh or dried grapes or anything that is produced by the grape vine. Their hair could not be cut for the days of their separation, nor could they touch a dead body. Because the men who participated in this vow were to grow their hair out long, it is argued by some that this is evidence against transcendent significance of 1 Corinthians 11:14–15.

The primary and most basic response to this argument is that men under a Nazirite vow were, in principle, an exception to what is natural. Under this vow, men and women were set apart by not being allowed to eat and drink certain foods or touching the dead. These actions, along with total abstinence from hair-cutting, were unnatural for both sexes; yet these actions set them apart for the God of Israel during the days of their vow. If exceptions among the Israelites are to be inferred as normative for the new covenant community, it could also be argued that Deborah's position as judge in Israel is evidence that women can have authority over men in the church, as many egalitarians teach.

Does the phrase "praying or prophesying" limit the covering instructions to the apostolic age?

Some believe that Paul's instructions regarding head covering were limited to the first century church because "praying and prophesying," as Paul had in view, is no longer occurring today. Since prayer is coupled with prophecy in the passage, some define "praying" as "praying in tongues." Those who believe the gift of tongues has ceased along with the gift of prophecy would see the head covering instruction as expiring with those gifts. Many issues converge in this interpretation, so a longer answer is required. Joe Rigney holds to this view and has articulated it this way:

My own view is that the fundamental issue in Paul's mind is how to maintain proper order and dignity in the corporate worship gathering in light of the extraordinary pouring out of the Holy Spirit on all of God's people...Paul is concerned that the fundamental order of reality is reflected in the actions, behavior, and appearance of men and women in the church, even when God's Spirit prompts a woman to pray or prophesy. In other words, Paul wants the Corinthian culture to reflect God's sacred order in a fitting and proper way. The use of head coverings by women when offering prayers or prophecy in the corporate gathering is a way of communicating, "The fact that I am publicly declaring God's words as spontaneously carried along by the Holy Spirit does not mean that I'm rebelling against God's sacred order."

Women prophesying and praying (in tongues) under the influence of the Holy Spirit seems to undermine that normal and natural order. The head covering is a symbol of authority that tells the world (and all who are watching, including the angels!) that the supernatural doesn't overthrow nature, but instead glorifies it. In first-century Corinth, the head covering was a culturally appropriate way of maintaining and celebrating the goodness of God's design in nature and Scripture.[7]

Proponents of this view often turn to 1 Corinthians 14:13–15 and note how Paul spoke of praying in tongues in that portion of the letter, arguing he had the same prayers in view in chapter 11. That passage is the only other time after chapter 11 where he mentioned prayer, and it is found within the context of exercising miraculous sign gifts. Therefore, some interpreters say that the type of prayer intended in the context of instructions about HCHL is the charismatic prayer in tongues, as Rigney parenthetically noted. To these commentators, the fact that prayer is joined with prophesying further emphasizes the concept that this is a charismatic prayer. Although this view is much more respectable than many other views of the HCHL text, it still falls short because it employs an abnormal method of Bible interpretation.

As mentioned, the only occurrences of "prayer" after chapter 11 are found in 14:13–15. Of these mentions, some have charismatic prayer in view and others do not. It reads, "Therefore let one who speaks in a tongue pray that he may interpret. For if I **pray in a tongue**, my spirit prays, but my mind is unfruitful. What is the outcome then? I will **pray with the**

---

[7] Joe Rigney, "What Makes a Man – or a Woman? Lost Voices on a Vital Question," Desiring God, https://www.desiringgod.org/articles/what-makes-a-man-or-a-woman, Accessed August 2022. Parenthetical phrases original.

spirit and I will pray with the mind also; I will sing with the spirit and I will sing with the mind also." The first and last mentions of prayer in this passage have to do with normal prayer in a language understood by the speaker. The middle mentions of prayer (in bold) have to do with charismatic praying in tongues.

Although it is important to recognize Paul's reference to praying in tongues in this portion of the letter, it is hardly a solid precedent for defining what Paul meant by "prayer" in chapter 11. Normal methods of biblical interpretation do not define the terms within a passage by reading ahead in the letter to see how those particular words are used in a different context. That information is always valuable and helpful, but it is never the precedent (after all, precedents should *precede*).

It is worth considering that the only other mention of prayer in 1 Corinthians is found in 7:5, and no commentator has sought to interpret Paul as intending the charismatic form of prayer. Furthermore, prayer is mentioned on its own in 11:13. If there is a case to be made that the "praying" of vv. 4–5 is praying in tongues because it is coupled with prophesying, v. 13 must still be dealt with.

Additionally, it should be recognized that Paul did not discuss the "extraordinary pouring out of the Holy Spirit" until 12:1, as signified by the introduction, "*Now concerning* spiritual gifts," (emphasis added). It is true that prophesying has in view the miraculous sign gift of prophecy, which, according to both Joe Rigney and this author, is not operative today in the same way as it was then; nevertheless, it is very significant that the apostle did not mention tongues or any other miraculous sign gifts in chapter 11. Those elements were not his focus. Neither the age of apostles nor miraculous sign gifts seem to be the basis of Paul's reasoning in any sense. Further evidence to consider is that Paul did not mention the covering again in the letter, even when he specifically addressed his desired order for prophesying in the assembly (14:29–38).

Thus, Rigney's interpretation could be summarized more accurately this way: "Paul is concerned that the fundamental order of reality is reflected in the actions, behavior, and appearance of men and women in the church [**only during the age of miraculous gifts and apostles**], when God's Spirit prompts a woman to pray [**in tongues**] or prophesy." Adding these elements in chapter 11 would give Paul a basis that he himself does not provide—a very dangerous proposition.[8] His claim that Paul gave this instruction so the church could show "that the supernatural doesn't overthrow nature" may be a fair summary statement of the apostle's concern, but it does not follow that it was only applicable to the first century when miraculous sign gifts were in operation. Even today, man is still the head of woman and angels are still beholding the corporate gathering of believers, all while women lead in praise, prayer, and other aspects of corporate worship.

---

[8] For more discussion about the type of prayer Paul had in view and what prophesying is, see "Personal Application of the Interpretation" on page 73.

Therefore, it could be said that if one is going to find a connecting theme between chapters 11 and 14, it should be that Paul was concerned with the order of the corporate gathering. Tongues and the exercising of charismatic gifts are not the key issue in chapter 11 as they are in chapter 14; however, the entire section of chapters 11–14 holds in common the concern for order in the assembly. The apostle desired God's order to be manifested while men and women participated in praying or prophesying (11:2–16), while the fellowship partook of the Lord's Supper (11:17–34), and while spiritual gifts were spontaneously exercised (ch. 12–14).

Another component of Rigney's interpretation is an emphasis of the instruction given to women over the instruction given to men. Granted, Paul used more words in the passage addressing the women, and the Corinthian women seem to have been particularly rebellious; however, men are addressed first (v. 4) and twice overall (v. 7). If Paul's purpose for the instruction was merely to call the women appear submissive while praying and prophesying in the gathered assembly, why were the men instructed to appear a certain way also?

Some might respond by claiming that Paul was setting up a point-counterpoint. If the women were to cover, it would be most natural for the men not to cover so that the woman's covering stood out. However, this understanding overlooks the fact that men were instructed first. If there is a complementary antithesis at play, the women fill that role in symbolizing their submission to their husbands. Additionally, Paul plainly stated that the basis of the initial instruction given to the men is a proper honoring of Christ (v. 4) as the image and glory of God (v. 7).

In his view, Rigney highlights some important facts of the matter in first-century Corinth. The church was new; miraculous sign gifts were being poured out by the Holy Spirit at a seemingly high rate; it is possible that there were no elders or deacons established there yet. It was an extremely unique time. But does it necessarily follow that these realities were what prompted Paul to give them this teaching?

The fact that Paul and the rest of the apostles taught this custom to all of God's churches (v. 16) indicates that these instructions applied to all the fellowships, regardless of the maturity of the church and details about the surrounding culture. If the shock of the newness of corporate worship in the church—particularly women playing a vital role in that worship—prompted this inspired passage, that "newness" certainly would not be limited to the exercising of certain gifts. Still today, women in the church serve, lead, and speak (read: pray) in ways that may cause some to think they have gone against nature. The symbol on their heads maintains its relevance, especially for the angels who continue to peer into the gathered assembly and behold the order upheld by the saints.

The church that Jesus is building is unlike any anything else that came before it. Men and women hold the priesthood equally, are indwelt and gifted by the Spirit, and participate in the same great commission. Yet, at the same time, gender distinctions exist, and these have implications for the roles people fill in the church. The covering instructions for men and women are still relevant.

If the covering is not defined, how could it continue to be observed rightly today?

It was noted above that a woman's hair is not her covering (see #11 in the first section). The vast majority of Bible interpreters recognize this point.[9] A good number of interpreters also recognize that the HCHL instruction was not based on cultural customs and that it was not limited to the age of charismatic sign gifts. Their objection to recognizing the application of head coverings in contemporary culture is that the fabric covering is not described or defined; thus, it would be impossible for women in the church today to practice head-covering rightly. Alistair Begg taught this view in a sermon from 1993:

> As to the precise nature of what the covering is, we've got to be honest enough to say that it is not clear. So, here we are at one of our fundamental principles of hermeneutics which is that the main things are the plain things and the

---

[9] In the fifth message of Milton Vincent's popular nine-part series on this passage, he noted that only seven of the 64 commentaries he consulted on 1 Corinthians claimed that a woman's hair is the covering Paul had in mind in vv. 5–6. Vincent taught that series in January–February 2002 and it can be found here: "Series: Head Coverings," Cornerstone Fellowship Bible Church, https://www.cornerstonebible.org/series/head-coverings, Accessed August 2022.

plain things are the main things. Now what is plain is that he wants women to be distinguishable from men and it has something to do with what they put on their heads. So, we know that, and we can debate all night whether it's a shawl or whether it's their hair or whatever else it is, but it doesn't affect the main issue…What is the application? Is the application of this to teach that women ought to return to wearing coverings or veils? No. We need to distinguish between the principle, which is timeless, and the application in a specific culture, which will vary.[10]

Like the Joe Rigney quote above, this view is more respectable than many others and the honesty of the struggle is to be appreciated. However, with all due respect (he's my favorite preacher!), Begg's reasoning falls short of sound biblical interpretation.

At a base level, and as an example, it is well-understood that communion, baptism, singing, giving, serving, praying, and reading Scripture are all practices that should be observed by the church in all ages. Although the details of each of these outward expressions may vary somewhat from culture to culture, the practices are to be retained as principles in and of themselves that the church must hold on to. If a culture does not understand

---

[10] From the sermon, "Man and Woman in Biblical Perspective – Part Two," (preached on September 19, 1993), Truth for Life, https://www.truthforlife .org/resources/sermon/man-woman-in-biblical-perspt2, Accessed August 2022.

baptism, generally rejects singing, or mocks the practice of praying, that does not change the church's call to observe them.

In the same way that "we've got to be honest" with the unknown material of the head covering that Paul had in mind, it should be confessed that the Bible does not specify the form of bread to use in communion, the type of water to use in baptism, or the style of corporate singing that should occur in the corporate gathering. Granted, there are questionable details unique to HCHL (see "The Unique Nature of the HCHL Instruction" on page 98), but the principle here is the same. The apostle's lack of detail in the text should lead believers to understand that there is freedom of expression in the practice rather than jumping to a cancellation of the practice altogether. In the same way all other New Testament practices are maintained in the church today even though there is some degree of detail missing, HCHL instruction should be held onto as well.

Adding to that, it is a frightening proposition to require from God a personal standard of clarity before having a willingness to obey. It is either pride or fear that would drive a person to tell God, "I must know all the details before I can obey." As stated in the introduction, willingness to obey the revelation of God should precede the interpretation of the revelation of God. The HCHL issue often serves to expose the disposition of each one's heart in this way.

Isn't this a matter of personal conviction?

There are different types of convictions in the Christian life. Some convictions are doctrinal in nature, derived from Scripture itself through an interpretive process. Other convictions are matters of conscience, defined by a believer's ability (or inability) to carry out an activity unbothered in spirit.

The HCHL instruction is not a conscience-conviction issue. Matters of conscience are, by definition, one of two things:

1. Activities that Scripture does not address in principle
2. Activities that Scripture says Christians are free to engage in, unless it cannot be carried out in faith (Romans 14:23)

Paul's HCHL instruction does not fit into either one of those categories. Instead, a person's interpretation of 1 Corinthians 11:2–16 should be a matter of hermeneutics, making it a doctrine-conviction issue rather than an opinion (cf. Romans 14:1). Therefore, a person cannot employ the excuse of conscience for not following the apostle's instruction; he must reason from the text.

For more information about primary and secondary doctrine, along with doubtful things/opinions, visit dotheology.com/chart.

Doesn't the church have more important items on her plate?

This rebuttal has to do with the varying levels of doctrinal pertinence in the church—and it is very true that some teachings in the Bible are more urgently important than others. For instance, if a Christian stands up on a plane headed for a crash landing to share one final message with the other passengers, he or she better not start elaborating on the correct understanding of head coverings in the church! The gospel must come forth first (1 Corinthians 15:3ff).

However, in answering this general objection, one must consider the state of the Corinthian church. Of all the churches of Paul's time, the Corinthians may have been the most rebellious and plagued by immature, sinful desires. It could be imagined that Paul would have simply written to them about the basics of the gospel, sanctification, and Christian unity; however, he wrote to them about head covering and hair lengths. This either means that this doctrine is a basic doctrine for Christians or that doctrines that are "beyond basic" are still important for immature fellowships. Perhaps it should be concluded that since this instruction was important for the Corinthians' worship, it remains important for the worship of believers in every culture today, too.

Is this worth the potential awkwardness and divisiveness in the local church?

The heart of this objection is likely very good and honorable. Psalm 133:1 states, "Behold, how good and how pleasant it is for brothers to dwell together in unity!" This sentiment is so true and all who have experienced true unity in the local church understand it very well. Unity among God's people is to be advocated at every turn and protected at all costs.

Another passage, Proverbs 27:17, says, "Iron sharpens iron, so one man sharpens another." This "sharpening" often comes in the form of disagreement and confrontation, causing sparks to fly at times. This, too, is good for the church. Unity in the church is not preserved by avoiding difficult topics or awkward situations. In fact, unity in the church is often fostered through such situations.

Ultimately, reclaiming the practice of HCHL is about obedience to God through the inspired word He has given the church. Any unity that is the result of ignoring the word of God is not Christian unity. Therefore, it is paramount that all Christians first submit to God and only then should they submit to one another (Ephesians 5:21). As a person (especially a woman) begins to observe the instructions found in 1 Corinthians 11 for the first time, there will certainly be awkward scenarios and conversations. A man cutting off his long hair of many years will certainly prompt questions from his friends. A woman's consistent covering at church might inspire some to gossip. Yet what matters most is that God is honored through obedience.

Regarding each one's responsibility before God, R.C. Sproul was cited earlier in this book as saying, "If I'm going to err, I'd rather err on the side of being overscrupulous of treating something that was a local custom as if it were a transcendent principle rather than ever being guilty of taking a transcultural principle of Almighty God and reducing it to a first-century custom."[11] This perspective is helpful. Believers need to be reminded of the importance of fearing God rather than man— and seeking to please Him above all others. Zac Poonen communicated this as well in a more direct way:

> If a sister is still in doubt about what this passage of Scripture teaches, let her consider this: Isn't it better for her to do more rather than less—and especially so when there is no inconvenience or cost involved? What will she lose by covering her head when she prays and prophesies? Nothing. But think of what she will gain by covering her head, if she discovers at the judgment-seat of Christ that this was indeed God's command? She will have the joy of having pleased her Lord on earth, in spite what other Christians taught and practised. So, every woman, if she

---

[11] Head Covering Movement, "What RC Sproul Believes About Head Covering," YouTube: https://youtu.be/X1Zmjyvet_4, Accessed August 2022.

is wise, will cover her head with a covering, when she prays and prophesies.[12]

If this is a law for the church, wouldn't disobedience require church discipline?

Two immediate responses should be given to this question. First, the HCHL instruction is not some sort of "law" for the church. Paul said that he was "under the law of Christ" (1 Corinthians 9:21), and defining that phrase is a challenge beyond the scope of this book. Yet it should simply be noted that the apostle was not giving the new covenant community a law—he never claimed to do that in any of his letters.

Second, what does or does not call for church discipline is actually a complicated conversation. Church discipline is the process of church members correcting other church members who are in sin. It is to be carried out through loving confrontation, following the process given by the Lord Jesus in Matthew 18:15–18. "Church Leadership Perspective" starting on page 91 is devoted to thinking through how the HCHL instructions should be encouraged in the fellowship and includes an extended consideration of church discipline. Regardless of whether or not a church should practice discipline on this issue, this question is not a legitimate objection to what the text says.

---

[12] "Head-Covering for Women - Zac Poonen," Sean Scott's Blog, https://preachingjesus.wordpress.com/2011/09/29/head-covering-for-women-zac-poonen, Accessed October 2022.

✦

It is difficult to see how careful and consistent exegesis could lead a Bible reader to believe that the apostle Paul did not intend for the HCHL instructions to be observed by the church in perpetuity. Sound principles of hermeneutics lead to the conclusion that the HCHL instructions remain for the contemporary church. As a test of one's own interpretive method, it may be helpful for the reader to ask himself, "Do I consistently approach all New Testament instruction this way?" Or, "Could I explain away the relevance of [baptism, fasting, giving, etc.] using the same level of scrutiny and the same hermeneutical approach I use in 1 Corinthians 11:2–16?"

In seeking to understand the HCHL issue as a culturally-conditioned encouragement from Paul, some believers have set unreasonable expectations for what the text should say in order for obedience to be required (see Steve Lawson's three requirements of the text on page 50). As faithful Bible students, we must aim for consistency in interpretation.

I hope it has been clearly seen that the various objections to this passage are not actually legitimate reasons to dismiss the HCHL instructions for the church. Once the text has been exegeted with normative interpretive principles and various objections to sound exegesis have been answered, all that is left is to apply the text.

Personal Application of the Interpretation

If you have made it this far and have agreed with my assessments, then you are a rare breed. As I'm sure you know, embracing the HCHL instruction is not popular or even widely supported within evangelicalism today. Bringing back this Scriptural custom is a very challenging task—and the *application* of the HCHL instruction is a key concern for those who desire to do it.

On page 67, I noted that the HCHL instruction is not a conscience-conviction issue, but rather a doctrine-conviction issue. This means that the overall continuing significance of the practice must be decided at the hermeneutics level, not the personal conscience level. However, as it pertains to what the specific personal application of the practice should *look like*, the apostle Paul did not issue grand detail; thus, many of the points of application must be approached as conscience-conviction aspects of the HCHL instruction.

Therefore, those who agree with the ongoing applicability of this passage will not all agree on the application for the church today. Certain forms of application have already been dismissed in this book (like women wearing coverings 24/7), but there are other forms that must not be dismissed so readily. In this section, application will be the main focus. Specific questions demand specific answers; however, not all points of application can be made with great confidence.

Before we mull over the sticking points of applying the passage today, we must pause to consider what exactly we are doing here.

To a certain degree, God has given all people an instinct to understand and do what is proper (see Romans 2:14–15). God's people, as the "called out ones," are, at a minimum, to recognize and embrace that which is natural. Beyond that, Christians have the Spirit of God and He leads us into spiritual understanding (1 Corinthians 2:10–16). By the power of the Spirit and the instruction of God's special revelation, the church is able to uphold and live out both the natural and the spiritual.

Thus, embracing the HCHL instruction is about more than just minding the word of God about hats and kerchiefs. It is about being faithful to the word of God for the sake of holiness in the church. Many would like to dismiss this passage and its application by laughing it off as some strange thing or a distraction from more important things, but we must consider this as a matter of faithfulness to the word of God, not some fascination with the abnormal. If your desire in exploring the application of this passage is simply to follow the rules, then you must reconsider your motivations. The ultimate desire for the church must be faithfulness to God, perfecting holiness in the fear of Him (2 Corinthians 7:1).

Which men did Paul have in view?

In 11:3, Paul states, "the man is the head of a woman." As noted earlier, there are reasons to believe that he had the husband-wife relationship in view in this phrase, as the ESV translation bears out. However, the initial phrase of the verse states that "Christ is the head of every man." The men spoken of in this verse could be all men—saved and unsaved—as the text says "every." Christ is the authority of all people in all generations; He is not merely the Lord of Christian husbands only. This interpretation seems legitimate.

In 11:4, Paul states, "Every man who has *something* on his head while praying or prophesying disgraces his head," (italics original). Understanding that Christ is the head of all men everywhere, it follows that all men are in view in this instruction. Since this instruction is very specifically pertaining to Christian activity, it is simply deduced that *Christian* men are to remove any head coverings when they pray or prophesy so as to honor Christ rightly. It is a challenging task to interpret the men of v. 4 as married Christian men only.

The question naturally follows, What constitutes a "man"? Is there an age at which a boy transitions to manhood? Are all males (even infants) in view? Scripture just does not give us that detail, so the reader must develop a conscience-conviction.

Which women did Paul have in view?

If all Christian men are being instructed in v. 4, does it follow that all Christian women are being instructed in vv. 5–6?

For the reasons given on pages 11-14, it seems best to understand the woman of v. 3 to be a married woman. Therefore, in 11:5, when Paul states, "Every woman who has her head uncovered while praying or prophesying disgraces her head," it seems most appropriate to understand that the uncovered woman is not honoring her husband rightly. This would rule out covering for girls, young women, and unmarried women.

There is an argument to be made that all females are in view here because, from the moment of birth, they have a functioning head in their father (cf. Numbers 30). This is not a bad argument, and it is worthy of further consideration.[1] If this view is taken, one must wonder, What about those women who have no living father or husband? Does male eldership in the local church also function as a "head" for women in that fellowship? Is there really a biblical case to consider all men to be the head of each woman throughout all of life generally?

The lack of conclusiveness on this point may be dissatisfying; the text stops where it stops.

---

[1] Consider Tertullian on this point: "It behooves our virgins to be veiled from the time that they have passed the turning-point of their age." David Garland adds: "[A woman's disorderliness] would reflect poorly on the particular men in the woman's life: her husband, father, or male head of the household. The husband is especially shamed when his wife uncovers her head in public," in *1 Corinthians* (Grand Rapids: Baker Academic, 2003), 522.

Which setting(s) did Paul have in view?

Paul did not specify with explicit terms any particular setting in which covering/uncovering for praying and prophesying applies. Because of this, there are many groups that consider the covering to be applicable anywhere and everywhere. Since believers are to "pray without ceasing" (1 Thessalonians 5:17), some apply the covering/uncovering principles as a 24/7 dress code. (Interestingly, very few, if any, groups refuse coverings to men on a 24/7 basis even when they encourage women to cover 24/7.) Despite the widespread disagreement on this issue, there are strong indications that limit the scope of Paul's view to the corporate worship gathering.

First, Paul had corporate gathering issues in view throughout the whole letter and continued this emphasis in the chapters that follow. One could say that the whole letter is about corporate holiness in the church. Paul spoke of divisions in the gathering (1:10ff), his visit with the gathering (2:1ff), illustrations for the gathering (3:9), Timothy's upcoming visit with the gathering (4:17), the need for discipline in the gathering (5:4–5), the need for judgment in the gathering (6:1ff), the benefit of undistracted devotion in the gathering (7:35), the exercise of liberty in the gathering (8–10), and the Lord's Table (10:14–22). Of course, not every instruction issued by Paul in the letter finds its application in corporate worship only; however, it must be recognized as a base observation that the context of the local church gathering explicitly permeates this letter. The word "church" appears more than twice as many times in this letter than in any other letter he penned.

Second, Paul praised the Corinthians for holding onto the traditions he delivered to them (11:2) and, later in the same chapter, he went on to withhold praise from them because they come together not for the better, but for the worse (v. 17). Paul used the same wording in both instances when he said, "I praise you all," with the addition of the negative Greek adverb *ouk* in the latter. A logical deduction may be made from his phrasing as he wrote back-to-back paragraphs, alternately praising and not praising, supposing that he had the same setting in mind. Clearly in 11:17 he was speaking to corporate worship practices when he said "you come together" and addressed the corporate observance of the Lord's Supper. When Paul said, "I praise you all" in v. 2, it is very possible that he was speaking to their corporate worship practices. John Murray, who believed in the continuing observance of the HCHL instruction, elaborated on this point in a letter to a presbytery in Australia:

> There is a distinct similarity between the terms of verse 17 and of verse 2. Verse 2 begins, "Now I praise you" and verse 17, "Now in this . . . I praise you not". The virtually identical expressions, the one positive and the other negative, would suggest, if not require, that both have in view the behavior of the saints in their assemblies, that is, that in respect of denotation the same people are in view in the same identity as worshippers. If a radical difference, that between private and public, were contemplated, it

would be difficult to maintain the appropriateness of the contrast between "I praise you" and "I praise you not."[2]

Third, Paul did not just speak to covering/uncovering during prayer, but also during prophecy. This indicates he had the corporate worship setting in view because New Testament prophesying was a practice that was unique to the gathered assembly. A person could not practice the gift of prophecy alone. As Jeremy Gardiner has written, "Sometimes we know *where* we're talking about by *what* we're talking about. If I mention taking the Lord's Supper, do you know where I'm talking about? Of course! The Lord's Supper is to be eaten when we meet together as a church. It's not something you practice in private. The same is [true] for prophecy."[3]

Fourth, Paul's mentioning of the angels' observance indicates the gathered assembly. All readers of this text readily admit that the mentioning of angels is ambiguous; however, it is not without purpose. The Bible explains that there are angels who long to look into Christian salvation (1 Peter 1:12) and that angels attend the gathered Christian assembly in heaven

[2] "The Use of Head Coverings in the Worship of God," Presbyterian Reformed Church, https://web.archive.org/web/20150204053945 /https://presbyterianreformed.org/1992/01/use-head-coverings-worship-god, Accessed August 2022.

[3] "Where are Head Coverings to be Practiced? In Church or Everywhere?", The Head Covering Movement, https://www.headcoveringmovement.com /articles/where-are-head-coverings-to-practiced-in-church-or-everywhere, Accessed August 2022.

(Hebrews 12:22). Thus, it could be understood that Paul's mentioning of angels is another indication that he had corporate worship in view.

Fifth, Paul's mentioning of "the [other] churches" (v. 16) indicates that the covering/uncovering instructions were practiced in the setting of the gathered local church. The apostle did not mention other individuals practicing the covering in constancy, but rather other churches who observed the practice together. It could rightly be said based on Paul's mentioning of churches here that the covering is a "church practice."

Sixth, the Corinthian church apparently had a particular problem with their women, who seemingly sought to throw off their God-given role in the church. Paul indicated this when he anticipated the retort of the Corinthians: "if one is inclined to be contentious…" (v. 16). His anticipation was not without cause. Later in the letter, Paul gave a direct instruction in this regard when he called the women to keep silent in the churches when it came to passing judgment on prophetic utterances (14:34–35). Thus, the instructions regarding HCHL were particularly pertinent to them as their women were often pushing back against God's structure in the gathered assembly.

Seventh, the lack of Old Testament precedent implies that this is a New Covenant corporate worship practice. Old Testament saints could certainly pray and prophesy—but they were never given any sort of instructions for covering/uncovering. What has changed? The mysterious age of the church has now been revealed with its unique ordinances in the assembly. Along with Sunday worship, water baptism, communion, singing to one another, conscience-driven giving, and the like, the instructions for covering/uncovering are set before the local church as a practice for gathered worship. Although the foundation for the covering instruction is rooted in God's created design for gender roles, the fact that the instruction was not given to any Old Testament saints as an individual prayer or prophesying practice indicates that it is for the local church's corporate worship.

Which prayers did Paul have in view?

Another point of application naturally arises: At what points in the corporate worship gathering is the covering instruction applicable? Are men and women only to uncover and cover when they are the ones leading others by praying out loud or does it apply at any point in the service when anyone is praying? Did Paul also have in view times of praise, since many worship songs are essentially prayers to God, and since Scripture often links the subjects of prayer, praise, and exhortation?

The first determination that must be made in this particular application is whether 1 Corinthians 14:34–35 negates the possibility of women speaking out loud at all in the gathered assembly. That passage reads, "The women are to keep silent in the churches; for they are not permitted to speak, but are to subject themselves, just as the Law also says. If they desire to learn anything, let them ask their own husbands at home; for it is improper for a woman to speak in church." Considering Paul's instruction here, John Calvin believed that the apostle never taught that women were allowed pray or prophesy in church, that he did not intend to commend such a practice in chapter 11.[4]

It seems much better to understand that Paul was allowing for women to speak in the church through the exercise of their spiritual gifts and in prayer (perhaps he had singing in mind as well), and that he was forbidding something else later in the epistle. The context of 14:34–35 is how the church should go about passing judgment on prophecies given. Paul noted that in the gathered assembly, each one came with a verbal contribution (14:26)—and that certainly included the women. From there, he gave instructions for the exercising of the miraculous sign gifts of tongues (vv. 27–28) and prophecies (vv. 29–33) as those particular contributions were realized in church.

---

[4] Calvin wrote, "It may seem, however, to be superfluous for Paul to forbid the woman to prophesy with her head uncovered, while elsewhere he wholly prohibits women from speaking in the Church (1 Timothy 2:12). It would not, therefore, be allowable for them to prophesy even with a covering upon their head...the Apostle, by here condemning the one, does not commend the other. For when he reproves them for prophesying with their heads uncovered, he at the same time does not give them permission to prophesy in some other way, but rather delays his condemnation of that vice to another passage, namely in 1 Corinthians 14. In this reply there is nothing amiss, though at the same time it might suit sufficiently well to say that the Apostle requires women to show their modesty—not merely in a place in which the whole Church is assembled, but also in any more dignified assembly, either of matrons or of men, such as are sometimes convened in private houses," (*Commentary on 1 Corinthians*, note on 11:5).

The apostle commanded the church to let only two or three prophets speak before letting "others pass judgment," (v. 29). This aspect of judging prophecies is the context for not only vv. 34–35, but through v. 38. Although certain women were enabled to prophesy (11:5, cf. Acts 21:9), no women were commissioned to judge the prophecies, as that is a teaching and discernment function in the church reserved for qualified men only (1 Timothy 2:11–12). All who had the gift were allowed to prophesy (1 Corinthians 14:31), but only men could judge the prophecies (vv. 29, 34–36), and their judgment was to be based on the inspired apostolic instruction (vv. 37–38). Paul was concerned about keeping this order (vv. 39–40).

From there, many different possibilities exist as to how the original question above may be answered, and there is no simple or certain way to settle the debate. The covering instructions in vv. 4–5 are for men and women to observe "*while* praying or prophesying" (emphasis added). It is likely that the apostle was speaking of times when the man or woman was leading in one of those ministries since it could not be said that one is "prophesying" if he or she is a silent onlooker. But is a person to be considered "praying" if someone else is leading and he or she is joining the leader in spirit? It seems impossible to arrive at certainty in answering that question.

In most church gatherings today, men will typically (and seemingly instinctively) uncover their heads for the entire meeting. In other situations, most men will uncover their heads any time a prayer is offered. A man's uncovered head is becoming less normal, though, as ballcaps seem especially fashionable for many of today's praise band members.

In some churches, women will cover their heads any time a prayer is offered. Most women who believe in the continuing significance of the HCHL instruction will remain covered for the entirety of the church meeting as a means of "covering bases." What exactly did Paul have in mind? A variety of detail questions exist when it comes to Scripture and this is one that simply cannot be answered with much certainty. The lack of detail in the text may leave many Bible readers unsatisfied; however, personal application can be made through the Spirit's leading into practical conviction.

What does it mean to prophesy?

In 1 Corinthians, Paul used the verb *propheiteuo* ("to prophesy") ten times: twice in chapter 11, once in chapter 13, and seven times in chapter 14. The word appears in the New Testament twenty-eight times, and the word means to either foretell or, in a spiritually gifted way, to put forth divine revelation authoritatively. This word does not simply mean "preaching."

It is a matter of Christian debate as to whether the spiritual gift of prophecy continues today. Either way, it is clear enough that some women in the first century church were able to prophesy through that special gifting (cf. Acts 21:9), and they were expected to cover their heads when they did so in the gathered assembly.

It is difficult to know how far to take the "praying or prophesying" events that Paul had in mind. As previously discussed, some interpreters limit the entirety of this activity to the first century. Some see the instruction to cover during prayer as applicable but believe prophesying has ceased. Others still regard the phrase "praying or prophesying" to be a catch-all phrase that pertains to all gathered fellowship activity and so the covering instructions are to be observed for the entirety of the gathering. Some people do not necessarily interpret the phrase that way but observe covering/uncovering for the entirety of corporate worship anyway for simplicity's sake.

What should a woman's head covering look like?

Paul gives no instruction about the design or shape of the head covering. Clearly, the apostle instructs the women to place this symbol on their heads (v. 10), but beyond that, the style is unclear. Some have made the case for a longer veil based on the verb *katakalupto* ("to cover") literally meaning in one sense, "down from the head."[5] This may indeed be what Paul had in mind, but he does not explicitly indicate that this was his concern. The word can also mean "down *on* the head."

It seems most reasonable for this aspect of the conversation to be considered a conscience issue. There will be many different

---

[5] Cleon L. Rogers Jr. and Cleon L. Rogers III, "First Corinthians," *The New Linguistic and Exegetical Key to the Greek New Testament* (Grand Rapids: Zondervan, 1998), 373.

styles of covering, just as there are many different styles of communion bread, baptism water, and clothes themselves. This is a wisdom issue, and a woman would do well to get godly counsel from mature Christian women.

Words of Encouragement

Human beings are complicated, and we tend to complicate everything we touch. Our limitations, when coupled with our fallen state, give birth to countless frustrations. I'm starting this final chapter this way because it is important for us to understand that few situations in life are as simple as we would like them to be.

Because of this reality, it would be unwise for those who embrace Paul's HCHL instruction to quickly accuse their fellow Christians of sin when they do not embrace the instruction. It is certainly possible that they are in sin, but that is not necessarily the case. Some believers may be fully convinced of an interpretation that relegates the applicability of 1 Corinthians 11 to the first century based on hermeneutics rather than culture. Some believers may have heard a convincing teaching on the passage that was erroneous, but they have simply never heard any other teaching. Then there may be some other believers who have just never engaged with the text.

Therefore, we must be very careful in our conversations with other Christians on this topic. In our dialogue, we must all be kind and tender-hearted (Ephesians 4:32), showing devotion to one another in brotherly love (Romans 12:10). The mutual goal must be to understand the text and follow God diligently.

It is also helpful to recognize that the HCHL issue is not the only one that has been mishandled by churches throughout the years. For example, there have been massive eras in church history when world missions were not emphasized, let alone practiced. This fact does not mean that all of those Christians were in sin or blatant rebellion. For many, they were simply never provoked to think about it.

In the same way, 1 Corinthians 11 has been the "hidden book" for many churches. Pastors have skipped it during their teaching through Paul's letter and laypeople have become accustomed to glossing over it in their personal reading. Multiple generations have stopped practicing the passage and this has made the whole ordeal more confusing for those who might have questions. Thus, the HCHL issue is covered with an array of bad practices, lazy thinking, and poor examples.

Yet, there can be renewal in the church. God will never be "finished" with His people. Until He returns, there will be endless opportunities for repentance, fresh obedience, and growth. Regardless of your situation, the Lord can use you to promote faithfulness in His church.

How should this happen? The best approach is to "outdo one another in showing honor," not being slothful but rather "fervent in spirit," (Romans 12:10, ESV). When fellow believers admonish one another while exemplifying the fruit of the Spirit, God is at work. To be sharpened by one another in patience, kindness, and gentleness is to be helped in Christian love. To "live in peace with one another" and to "be patient with everyone" (1 Thessalonians 5:13–14), even amid a strong disagreement, is to reflect the love of Christ by which God will work.

Therefore, do not grow weary of doing good (Galatians 6:9, 2 Thessalonians 3:13). Seek the Lord and the purity of His church. Fear Him above all else and, in love, be willing to help others understand what He has said. May God grant you great strength for His work.

Church Leadership Perspective

Insistency vs. Flexibility

If you are a church leader and have become convinced that there is continuing significance and application of 1 Corinthians 11:2–16 for today, you are suddenly approaching a moment of crisis. "How will I explain this to my church?" you might wonder. "Will they follow?" or, perhaps more importantly, "How should I respond if they disagree with me?"

Church leaders who conclude that the HCHL instructions found in 1 Corinthians 11 are for today must answer the question, "How will these principles be brought to bear on the local church?" There is no easy answer to that question. If there is a *right* practice and a *wrong* practice for men and women, how will the wrong practices be addressed? How will the right practices be encouraged? Is this a sin issue? Should local church leadership insist on the membership upholding a certain practice?

To begin to answer the question, it seems helpful to zoom out and see the big picture, even setting aside the HCHL topic for the sake of a thought exercise.

91

Drawing Lines

When considering local church leadership's "enforcement" or "insistency" on any given issue, it is perhaps simplest—hopefully not *simplistic*—to consider two categories: announced doctrine and formal insistency. **Announced doctrine** is the stated position of a local church or one of its leaders on an issue, made known to all. **Formal insistency** is the enforcement or prohibition of a behavior or belief by way of church discipline, often initiated by the leadership. As stated earlier in this book, church discipline is the process of church members correcting other church members who are in sin. It is to be carried out through loving confrontation, following the process given by the Lord Jesus in Matthew 18:15–18. *Not all matters of announced doctrine become matters of formal insistency in the local church.*

Announced doctrine may cover a very broad range of topics as found in the official doctrinal statement, sermons, lessons, books, and other media. Some churches seek to keep their announced doctrine generally basic, often limiting it to just the definitional aspects of Christianity (Apostles' or Nicene Creed, etc.), while other churches have very extensive doctrinal statements. Either way, churches have doctrinal convictions they make known to others through various means, and these function as markers to show where the church or the leadership stands on certain issues.

Formal insistency rarely matches with announced doctrine at a 1:1 ratio for local churches that have doctrinal statements going beyond the "bare minimum" of basic doctrines. In fact, it could be said that if a church is formally insistent on all articles about which they have announced their doctrinal convictions, they have made themselves cult-like. So, herein lies a principle: *Not every publicly stated doctrine-conviction of a church or its leadership should be enforced by way of church discipline.*

Thus, the majority of cases in which a local church member is disciplined tend to fit into three categories: (1) rejection of a definitional doctrine of Christianity, (2) divisiveness in the body, and/or (3) blatant personal lifestyle sins of commission.[1]

The first two categories are easy enough to understand. For example, if Joe Smith at First Baptist Springfield started to believe that infants should be baptized, and subsequently ran around the church seeking to convert members to his side (causing division), he would be confronted and disciplined quickly and directly—and rightly so. The same action would take place if it turned out that Joe, who had been a member for twenty-five years, suddenly rejected the inerrancy of Scripture (a definitional doctrine of Christianity).

---

[1] Since drawing up these three categories, I have found other authors who basically agree with my analysis. D.A. Carson says that there are "three areas that could lead to the supreme sanction, excommunication: [a] flagrantly immoral life, major doctrinal aberration, and a loveless, fundamentally divisive spirit," in *Showing the Spirit* (Ada: Baker Books), 246. Gary Inrig gives four categories: open sexual immorality, unresolved personal conflicts, divisiveness, and false teaching in *Life in His Body* (Wheaton: Harold Shaw, 1975), 146.

But consider this: there is another Joe Smith at another First Baptist Springfield who loves his church and would never want to divide them. He is also totally orthodox in his theology. But this Joe regularly looks at pornography and does not seem to be able to get this behavior under control. This is a blatant personal lifestyle sin of commission—he is doing something he should not do.

Should that leadership of his church confront and discipline him as quickly as the other church would deal with the other Joe? It depends, of course. Is there evidence that he is seeking to fight the sin? Has he made some improvements through devotion to God and accountability to the church? Has anyone even taken the time to explain the issues to him? This type of situation is not easy to resolve; nevertheless, this kind of scenario is the third main category that prompts formal insistency (church discipline) in the local body.

Omission Leading to Flexibility

Situations get all the more confusing when dealing with sins of *omission*, as opposed to the more blatant and obvious sins of *commission*. If Sally Jones at Second Baptist Springfield was baptized as a newborn in the Presbyterian tradition and does not feel the need to be baptized as an adult believer, church leadership is faced with an interesting quagmire. Does their **announced doctrine** become **formal insistency** on this matter? As Southern Baptists, it is likely that believer's baptism is a requirement for membership at Second Baptist, so the leadership could dismiss Sally's case easily enough by withholding membership from her according to the Bylaws. Since church discipline is reserved for members at SBC Springfield, they can avoid going down that road altogether.

Whew, that was a close one.

But what about Susan Martinez? She has been a member of Second Baptist for thirty years, but she refuses to take communion. She certainly calls herself a Christian (and she has the believer's baptism certificate to prove it!), but she sees no need to continue the New Testament practice of consuming the elements of bread and wine (actually, it's grape juice; these are Baptists, after all). Many people in the church are aware of Susan's abstinence from communion, but she maintains her conviction. Should the church's **announced doctrine** regarding the ordinance of communion be handled with **formal insistency** in this case, correcting Susan through the stages of church discipline? Should she be removed from the body for this sin of omission?

But wait, it gets more confusing!

Susan's adult son Robert gladly participates in communion—he believes it is right and biblical. However, Robert does not sing with the rest of the church during corporate worship. As everyone else stands to join in with the praise band or the hymn leader, Robert often remains seated, or otherwise stands silently. He does not like singing and he sees very little significance in it as presented in the Bible. Recently, Pastor Bud preached through Colossians 3 and Robert heard that it is good and right for local believers to sing songs, hymns, and spiritual songs together. However, Robert remains unconvinced since there are just two New Testament verses about it from one biblical author. How should church leadership respond?

These are not simple situations.

Those who have served in local church ministry know that Joe Smith, Sally Jones, Susan and Robert Martinez, and Pastor Bud are all real people. They are hypothetical for the purpose of this book, but they are most definitely real. Local church ministry is messy, difficult, confusing, and imperfect.

Hypothetical scenarios like the ones presented above are virtually endless. Consider a few more examples.

- The phrase "20% of church members do 80% of the work" has basically become gospel truth in most American churches because it is undeniable that many Christians abstain from serving the body the way they should.
- Joining a church in formal membership is becoming rarer, because more and more Christians are abstaining from a true commitment to the local assembly.
- Jesus taught that His disciples would fast (Mark 2:20), but very few churches have any sort of insistency on that issue—formally or actually.

- ◆ Women are to dress modestly and discreetly (1 Timothy 2:9), but very few churches are willing to even define what that means, let alone insist upon it.[2]
- ◆ Most church leaders are not only unaware of how much people give, but if people even give *at all*.

Individual local churches have to determine case-by-case how much flexibility will be offered in areas like these, where there is *omission* of an action. The reality is that the vast majority of churches have already decided (albeit subconsciously) that personal freedom in these areas is to be prioritized among body members. Strict formal insistency often gives way to freedom of personal application and expression, or, in some cases, even the freedom to openly disagree with the announced doctrine of the church. There are not a few doctrines and practices that local churches must face, deciding whether a doctrinal position should be announced or if formal insistency should be implemented. Each case comes with its own unique set of briars.

With all of that said, it should start to become obvious how the HCHL issue fits into the local church picture.

---

[2] For an interesting and entertaining article on how churches should deal with a woman's modesty or lack thereof, check out Doug Wilson's (I know, I know) article, "Evangelical Spandex at the Gym" on Blog & Mablog: https://dougwils.com/books-and-culture/books/evangelical-spandex-at-the-gym.html, Accessed November 2022.

The Unique Nature of the HCHL Instruction

There is a unique combination of features found in the HCHL instruction that make it difficult to apply to the local church from a leadership perspective. Consider the factors that come together on this issue:

- The covering is a *physical outward expression* for the *specific activity* of "praying and prophesying."
- Covering details are a bit ambiguous with respect to the *women* who are to observe the instruction.
- Covering/uncovering is a *regular practice* for believers, unlike the one-time event of baptism.
- Covering/uncovering is an *every-gathering practice* likely observed multiple times per week in most contexts, unlike communion, which is observed weekly at most by the majority of evangelical churches.
- Observance of hair lengths is for *all of life*.
- HCHL does not reflect the central events of the cross or resurrection, but it *uniquely reflects God's design for authority*.

Beyond these points, the HCHL instruction is often quickly dismissed in today's culture because it directs a person how to dress or appear in a public gathering. There is a presupposition of individual sovereignty in the minds of many Westerners and, consequently, there are varying levels of willingness when it comes to receiving instructions about clothing. This one aspect sets the HCHL issue apart from not only baptism and communion, but also singing, giving, praying, and a whole host of practices and traditions. The most comparable issue in this regard is the modest dress instruction directed toward Christian women (1 Timothy 2:9–10, 1 Peter 3:3–4).

When considering all of these factors, it becomes difficult for church leadership to determine how the HCHL issue should be insisted upon. Will a man be allowed to speak in the service while wearing a hat? Will the praise band guitarist be asked to cut his long hair? Are the women going to be handed bonnets on their way into the building? (Don't do that.)

Although the HCHL issue is unique, it is not uniquely *difficult*. The variety of ministry activities that take place within the local church are all capable of presenting daunting and undesirable situations. Consider the table at the end of this chapter, featuring other aspects of Christian living pertaining to the fellowship of the local church. Each of these has the potential for difficulty.

Local church leaders must wrestle with these issues and decide if it is appropriate to move a situation from mere **announced doctrine** to **formal insistency** when those they shepherd abstain from certain practices. At times, local church leaders will disagree on these issues among themselves. These disagreements are not just limited to how they should go about insisting on certain practices, but how to define them and even whether they should be seen as relevant for today or not. For example, fasting is often omitted from the believer's life and many Christians do not *feel* the need to observe it, though there is a broad and strong foundation for it. It is likely that church leaders will not agree how to present, encourage, and insist upon fasting; however, it is their duty to work through the issues together.

How much flexibility should be given to the congregation?

The leaders God has given to each congregation must decide.

	Some freedom in methodology generally given	All Christians expected to participate	Regularly practiced together	Not generally regarded as an ordinance	Spirit-led individual expression	Often practiced secretly	Rarely insisted upon by church leadership
Baptism	X	X					
Communion	X	X	X				
Singing	X	X	X	X	X		X
Giving	X	X	X	X	X	X	X
Membership*	X		X**	X			X
Praying	X	X	X	X	X	X	
Serving	X	X	X	X	X	X	X
Fasting	X	X		X	X	X	X
Modesty	X	X	X	X	X		X
HCHL	X		X	X	X		X

*Some churches do not have formal membership, but most who do have certain requirements such as age, baptism, regular attendance for a minimum amount of time, etc.

**Although this is not "practiced" in a particular way in the gathered assembly, it is still observed since there are individuals present who are official members and others who are not.

Appendix A:
Doctrines Based on One or Two Passages

One of the most common reasons for rejecting the ongoing significance of 1 Corinthians 11:2–16 is that the instruction appears in only one place in the New Testament. Even though transcendent foundations are provided for the practice and that all the other churches Paul knew also engaged in the practice, it remains that there is just one passage that speaks to this issue. Jesus did not teach on it; the early church is not described as observing it in the book of Acts; Paul was the only New Testament author to speak of it.

Is this reality sufficient grounds for the church to ignore Paul's instructions in this passage? The answer is a resounding *No!* In fact, if Christians were to pause and consider the number of doctrines they hold to that are supported primarily by one or two passages, the "one passage only" objection would quickly melt away.

Clearly, God does not intend for His people to develop an understanding of doctrinal rank and authority based on the number of appearances made by a certain teaching in Scripture. It is true that the more times a certain theme appears in the Bible, the clearer it typically becomes. However, this is not always the case. As will be seen below, there are certain doctrines that Christians hold dear even though God's revelation of them is somewhat minimal.

The following list of one- and two-passage doctrines should serve as a helpful inventory for the Christian considering whether or not God should have to reveal something a certain number of times before people are obligated to believe and obey.

One-Passage Doctrines

Length of the Messianic kingdom. Regardless of a person's interpretation, Revelation 20:1–6 is the only passage where Jesus' earthly kingdom is said to be 1,000 years in duration.

Qualifications for deacons. The required characteristics of deacons are only found in 1 Timothy 3:8–13.

Trinitarian baptism formula. Matthew 28:19–20 is the only passage where the church is instructed to baptize disciples "in the name of the Father and the Son and the Holy Spirit."

Caring for true widows. Paul instructs church leadership in how to care for widows in the church in just one passage: 1 Timothy 5:3–16.

Seriousness of idleness. Most Christians know the phrase, "If anyone is not willing to work, then he is not to eat, either." This phrase is only found once in the Bible and it is in the only New Testament instruction regarding idleness in the church, found in 2 Thessalonians 3:6–13.

Husbands' prayers being hindered. Just one verse indicates that a husband's prayer life will suffer harm if he refuses to live with his wife in an understanding way (1 Peter 3:7). However, it is of utmost importance that husbands heed those words!

Accusations against elders. It is crucial that no charge be brought against an elder unless there are two or three witnesses; yet, 1 Timothy 5:19 is the only verse that states this explicitly.

Believers suing each other. Many people recognize 1 Corinthians 6 as the "lawsuits chapter" of the New Testament—and it is the only such one.

Abandonment as grounds for divorce. In the next chapter of 1 Corinthians, the church is provided the only passage that speaks to the abandonment of a spouse as grounds for divorce (7:15).

Elect angels. It is a bit obscure, and it stands alone. First Timothy 5:21 is the only passage that tells us that the angels who did not follow Satan were preserved because they were chosen by God.

Jesus' high priestly prayer. John 17 is the only chapter in all of the gospels that records Jesus' amazing prayer on behalf of His disciples. Can you imagine if we discounted it (and the other unique accounts of Jesus' life found in the gospel of John) just because there is only one account of it? In this chapter, we have the only indication that Jesus prayed for future generations of believers (v. 20).

Instructions about communion. Ironically, 1 Corinthians 11 also provides the church with the only instruction for how the

Lord's Supper should be observed in the church. The New Covenant was initiated with Jesus' blood (Luke 22:20) and He illustrated this with the last Passover meal He enjoyed with His disciples. After the New Covenant was initiated and He began building His church, 1 Corinthians 11 was written.

The existence of certain spiritual gifts. The only place in the Bible where the gifts of administration, discernment, healing, tongues, interpretation of tongues, words of wisdom, words of knowledge, faith, helps, and miracles are mentioned is 1 Corinthians 12–14.

Two-Passage Doctrines

Corporate singing in the assembly. Ephesians 5:18–19 and Colossians 3:16 are the only two passages that instruct the church to sing together.

Office of deacon. Only two New Testament passages clearly indicate an office of deacon in the local church: Philippians 1:1 and 1 Timothy 3:8–13. Seven table-servers were appointed in Acts 6, and some people consider that passage to also speak of the office of deacon in the local church.

Sunday corporate worship. In Acts 20:7 and 1 Corinthians 16:2 there is indication that the church should gather for corporate worship on the first day of the week. In Revelation 1:10, John calls this day "the Lord's Day."

Steps of church discipline. There is only one New Testament passage that details the steps of church discipline in a protocol format, found in Matthew 18:15–18, and spoken by the Lord Jesus Himself. In Titus 3:10, the young church leader was given one more piece of instruction: "Reject a factious man after a first and second warning." Some may consider 1 Timothy 5:20 in this conversation also.

Moral obligation to pay taxes. Two passages outline the Christian duty to give money to the government in the form of taxes: Matthew 22:15–22 and Romans 13:6–7.

The office of evangelist. In only one New Testament passage is the office/gift of evangelist mentioned explicitly (Ephesians 4:11). Philip was called an evangelist (Acts 21:8), perhaps hinting at the office. Other than that, Timothy was told to "do the work of an evangelist" (2 Timothy 4:5) and that is the only other instance of the word in the Bible.

Qualifications for elders. Making sure elders in the church are duly qualified is very important. However, there are only two passages (1 Timothy 3:1–7 and Titus 1:5–9) that guide local churches in this endeavor.

Christian bema seat judgment. Christians will not be present at the Great White Throne judgment. Instead, believers will stand before the judgment seat of Christ. This reality is only revealed in Romans 14:10 and 2 Corinthians 5:10.

The "catching up" of Christians alive at Christ's coming. Regardless of what a person may think of the pre-tribulation rapture doctrine, there are only two passages that speak of the mystery of Christians being caught up together with Christ. These passages are John 14:3 and 1 Thessalonians 4:15–18.

✦

With all of these references in view, and considering the importance of these passages, how could we ever say that 1 Corinthians 11:2–16 should be ignored or chalked up to "mystery" because it is unique? Many passages are unique but, if they are in the Bible, they are inspired and authoritative!

Appendix B:
Voices from Church History[1]

"Woman and man are to go to church decently attired...for this is the wish of the Word, since it is becoming for her to pray veiled...Because of the angels, let her be veiled."

Clement of Alexandria

(150–215)

The Instructor, Book 3

"It behooves our virgins to be veiled from the time that they have passed the turning-point of their age... This observance is exacted by truth."

Tertullian

(155–220)

On the Veiling of Virgins

---

[1] A big "thank you" is owed to my friend Aaron Shafovaloff for his work in compiling and sharing many of these quotes.

"It is not becoming, even in married women,
to uncover their hair, since the apostle commands
women to keep their heads covered."

Augustine

(354–430)

Letter 245

"It pertains to a man's dignity...not to wear a covering on his
head...to show that he is immediately subject to God;
but the woman should wear a covering to show that
besides God she is naturally subject to another."

Thomas Aquinas

(1225–1274)

Commentary on 1 Corinthians

"[Paul's] traditions were the gospel of Christ, and honest
manners and living, and such a good order as becometh the
doctrine of Christ: as that a woman obey her husband,
have her head covered, keep silence, and
go womanly and Christianly appareled..."

William Tyndale

(1494–1536)

*Doctrinal Treatises and Introductions to
Different Portions of the Holy Scriptures, Vol. 1*

"If a woman prays or prophesies in the solemn assembly with
her head uncovered, she shames her head, because it ought to

be uncovered in private for the sake of her husband—not in a public assembly, where Christ is served, not her husband."

Desiderius Erasmus

(1466–1536)

Paraphrase of 1 Corinthians 11 as cited in
Reformation Commentary on Scripture, Vol. 9, 1 Corinthians

"The wife wears a symbol of authority, that is, the veil on her head, as St. Paul writes in 1 Corinthians 11, that she is not free but rather is under obedience to her husband. The wife veils herself with a fine, soft veil, spun and made from pretty, soft flax or linen…"

Martin Luther[2]

(1483–1546)

A Sermon on Marriage (1525) as cited in
Reformation Commentary on Scripture, Vol. 9, 1 Corinthians

"He now maintains from other considerations, that it is unseemly for women to have their heads bare. Nature itself, says he, abhors it. To see a woman shaven is a spectacle that is disgusting and monstrous…

---

[2] For more on Luther's views regarding the covering (and interesting artwork of his wife) see Jeremy Gardiner's "What Did Martin Luther Believe About Head Covering?", The Head Covering Movement, https://www.headcoveringmovement.com/articles/what-did-martin-luther-believe-about-head-covering, Accessed October 2022.

Should any one now object, that her hair is enough, as being a natural covering, Paul says that it is not, for it is such a covering as requires another thing to be made use of for covering it."

John Calvin
(1509–1564)
Commentary on 1 Corinthians

"'For this cause ought the woman to have power,' that is a covering, 'on her head, because of the angels'...
Methinks, holy and beloved sisters, you should be content to wear this power or badge."

John Bunyan
(1628–1688)
A Case of Conscience Resolved
(Women's Prayer Meetings)

"'But if it be a shame for a woman to be shorn or shaven...'
As it is accounted in all civilized nations: the very Heathens speak of it as a thing abominable, and of which there should not be one single dreadful example. Then let her be covered; with a veil, or any sort of covering in common use."

John Gill
(1697–1771)
Commentary on 1 Corinthians 11:6

"If a woman is not covered—if she will throw off the badge of
subjection—let her appear with her hair cut like a man's.
But if it be shameful for a woman to appear thus in public,
especially in a religious assembly, let her, for the same reason,
keep on her veil."

John Wesley

(1703–1791)

Notes on the Bible

"The reason why our sisters appear in the house of God with
their heads covered is 'because of the angels.' The apostle says
that a woman is to have a covering upon her head, because of
the angels, since the angels are present in the assembly
and they mark every act of indecorum, and therefore
everything is to be conducted with decency and
order in the presence of the angelic spirits."

Charles Spurgeon

(1834–1892)

Sermon titled "Another and Nobler Exhibition"

"I come into the presence of God and Christ and of the angels
who are learning the wisdom of God in the church,
and I remove my hat. For the same reason when a woman
comes into the church, she keeps her hat on."

H.A. Ironside

(1875–1951)

Addresses on the Song of Solomon

"Because the woman has not been given rule and headship her head must be covered, and covered with a double cover…When she comes into the house of God there must be the additional covering of the hat because she is also in subjection to her spiritual brethren to whom God has appointed rule."

A.W. Pink

(1886–1952)

Studies in the Scriptures, Vol. 5

"A woman should have her head covered to show that she is under the authority of the man…The Scripture teaches that when you and I are met as we are at this moment and when we're met together in prayer that the angels of God are present and are looking upon us. And the woman is to be covered when she takes part in public prayer because of the presence of the angels. It's a tremendous and a remarkable thing. Let us bear it in mind."

Martyn Lloyd-Jones

(1899–1981)

Sermon titled "Good Angels"

"So, every reason that Paul gives for the head covering is not cultural and yet evangelicals frequently say, 'Oh well, that's a cultural thing; we don't have to pay any attention to it.' The reasons are not cultural. Creation. Woman's hair itself. Nature itself. Angelic beings are looking down upon us. Those

are not cultural reasons. The apostle…I wish he were here.
'Isn't that right Paul?' 'Yes, that's right Lewis;
you're right that time, at least.'"

S. Lewis Johnson

(1915–2004)

Sermon titled "Covering the Head in Worship"

"This makes it the more necessary to ask the question whether
Paul is here simply dependent on custom, so that 'in
communities where it is no longer a disgrace for a woman to
"shorn," the argument has lost its point,' (Hooker, N.T.S.
x410…). This is probably not so; Paul thinks that nature
(see verse 14) expects a woman to be covered, so that
for her to be uncovered is not only an offense against custom
but also an unnatural act."

C.K. Barrett

(1917–2011)

Commentary on 1 Corinthians

"Women should be veiled or covered in the meeting of the
church, and the men should not. Paul's reasons were based on
theology (headship v. 3), the order of creation (v. 7–9), and the
presence of angels in the meeting (v. 10). None of these reasons
was based on contemporary social custom."

Charles Ryrie

(1925–2016)

The Ryrie Study Bible

"A woman who prays or prophesies in an assembly of believers should cover her head as a symbol of her submission to the absolute will of God who has ordered His universe according to His own good pleasure."

Bruce Waltke

(1930–)

"*1 Corinthians 11:2–16: An Interpretation,*"
in *Bibliotheca Sacra 135* (1978)

"Paul gives a reason. And if there is anything that is trans-cultural it is that which is rooted and grounded in creation. The reason he gives for this is rooted and grounded in creation, so I think it is a mistake to just dismiss that as a contemporary custom that is not applicable today. I'm in a minority on that point, remember. I give the minority report there."

R.C. Sproul

(1939–2017)

***Theology in Dialogue Conference* (2016)**